RELATIONSHIP GOALS
CHALLENGE

COMPANION TO THE #1 *NEW YORK TIMES* BESTSELLER

RELATIONSHIP GOALS CHALLENGE

30 DAYS FROM GOOD TO GREAT

MICHAEL TODD

with Eric Stanford

WATERBROOK

To my parents, Tommy and Brenda Todd, who challenged me,
loved me, and pushed me toward my wildest dreams.

Thank you for the tools and for being my example
of *real relationship goals.*

Forty-one years and counting . . .

#RelationshipGoals has been a trending topic worldwide for years now. Search for this hashtag on social media, and you'll find celebrity couples posing at exclusive clubs, stills from romantic movies at the point where the boy gets the girl, cute couples kissing on a beach or cuddled up in bed, a boyfriend-girlfriend pair holding balloons in the park and giving the impression that their relationship has never been anything but pure happiness. And when people repost these pictures with the hashtag, what are they saying? They're saying, "I want a relationship like that!" Kim and Kanye, Jay and Bey, Prince William and Kate, some unidentified couple who look really good in a picture that happened to go viral—we can easily become obsessed with their seemingly perfect images and make them our idols and ideals.

Okay, maybe you've never noticed #RelationshipGoals online, much less posted anything with it. But if I were to ask you to think about the relationship you want, would an idealized picture flash into your mind? Maybe it's you with a tall, handsome pro athlete who takes you on shopping sprees. Or maybe it's you beside a girl who's hood like Cardi B but has a sweet side like Carrie Underwood. Is he an amazing listener with a classic swag like George Clooney and a job that pays both his bills and yours? Can she cook like your mama and get just as hype as you do when your team scores?

Now, if you just asked *What's wrong with that?* in your

head, allow me to submit to you that maybe there's more to relationship than what pop culture has taught us or our own imaginings have dreamed up. Maybe our society sells an illusion of romantic relationship that's more like a mirage—the closer you get to it, the more you realize it's not real at all. Maybe the things we tend to celebrate are built on unstable foundations and are bound to eventually fall. But also . . . maybe there are some truths here that can be unlocked about how and why human connection is so important and how we can achieve it.

I believe so, and that's why I've written *Relationship Goals* . . . about *real* relationship goals.

—from *Relationship Goals*

CONTENTS

ACCEPT THE CHALLENGE   xiii

PURPOSE 1

DAY 1 | INVITE HIM IN   3

DAY 2 | THIRSTY FOR GOD   7

DAY 3 | YOU ARE WHO GOD SAYS YOU ARE   11

DAY 4 | DON'T FULFILL YOUR POTENTIAL   15

DAY 5 | SAY YES   19

DAY 6 | YOUR INNER CIRCLE   23

DAY 7 | SPEAK IT INTO BEING   27

DAY 8 | SINGLE IN A COUPLE   31

DAY 9 | PERMISSION TO PURSUE   35

DAY 10 | RE-PRESENTING CHRIST'S LOVE   39

HEALING 43

DAY 11 | A WORLD OF TROUBLE   45

DAY 12 | HOPE FOR YOUR HURDLES   49

DAY 13 | DOUBT INTERVENTION   53

DAY 14 | HERE'S MUD IN YOUR EYE   57

DAY 15 | DAMAGED GOODS   61

DAY 16 | GO TO THE MANUFACTURER   65

DAY 17 | THE SECRET TO JOY   70

DAY 18 | SAYIN' IT SWEET LIKE HONEY   74

DAY 19 | EPIC RECOVERY AFTER AN EPIC FAIL   78

DAY 20 | PICKING UP AFTER YOU WERE LET DOWN   82

ONENESS 87

DAY 21 | THE COMMUNITY AROUND THE COUPLE   89

DAY 22 | GET H.O.T.   94

DAY 23 | GIVE IT UP   98

DAY 24 | LOVE SPOKEN HERE   102

DAY 25 | FIGHTING FOR UNITY   105

DAY 26 | KINGDOM COWORKERS   109

DAY 27 | INVESTMENT IN LOVE   114

DAY 28 | COMMITTED TO THE RIDE   118

DAY 29 | NEVER PAUSE ON PURSUIT   122

DAY **30** | **YOU'RE SO FRESH!**   126

GO LIST   131

DAY **31** | **BONUS CHALLENGE**   135

ACCEPT THE CHALLENGE

Since my book *Relationship Goals* came out, I've been hearing from people all around the country and overseas about how it's helping them turn their lives away from the shallow #RelationshipGoals they used to pursue and start aiming for the kinds of relationships that will help them live out a purposeful life. I've heard from teenagers who have never even been on a date and from couples who have been married for decades, from longtime churchgoers and from people who are far from God, and many more. They're seeing change in their lives. They're rediscovering love and unity in their relationships and being liberated to do what they were put on this planet to do.

It's not because I'm so smart that these results are happening. (I've still got a lot to learn about relationships. Just ask my wife, Natalie.) What's making the difference is that *Relationship Goals* is based on the Word of God, which was true long before social media existed and will be true long after anybody remembers what a hashtag is.

I'm so thankful God has allowed me to play some part in helping to turn around some relationships. But there *is* one request I've been getting a lot, and that is for help to put the key principles of *Relationship Goals* into practice over the long term. In other words, to create new habits that will solidify gains and prevent relationships from slipping back to the way they were before.

That's where this book comes in.

Included are thirty Scripture-based messages that each end in a specific GO challenge—something for you to talk about or plan or do to improve your relationship. If you'll do one GO challenge per day, that's a month of new insights, key decisions, and fresh starts. Challenging, yes, but if you accept the challenge, it will help you meet your goals and win at relationship. It will take your relationship from good to great.

THE WORD OF GOD: TRUE LONG BEFORE SOCIAL MEDIA EXISTED AND STILL TRUE LONG AFTER ANYBODY REMEMBERS WHAT A HASHTAG IS.

I deliberately applied my book *Relationship Goals* to all kinds of important relationships in our lives, including friendships, work relationships, and church relationships. It was for people who are single and for people who are involved in romantic relationships. This book, however, is more focused. Here I'm specifically talking to people who are in a romantic relationship and want to make it better.

So, let me ask . . .

Are you dating? You're having fun hanging out with people and (I hope) exploring whether a particular person might be a godly marriage partner for you.

Or are you engaged? The big day is coming up. And meanwhile, maybe you're thinking that before you enter the covenant of marriage, it would be a good idea to make sure the two of you are aligned with each other and aligned with God.

Or are you married (whether for the first time, second time, or so on)? I don't care if you're all glowing with newlywed bliss or you've been married for forty years and you think you know what the other person is going to say before she does. Married people need to shake up the status quo to seize what God has for them.

If you're in any of those categories, this book is for you.

You're not going to find much advice in here like "Stick a love note in his pocket for him to find later" or "Buy your wife flowers on the way home from work." That's all fine, but you can come up with stuff like that on your own. Am I right?

The thirty-day *Relationship Goals Challenge* gets into substantial issues. It's going to help you find answers to questions like these:

- How does our love relationship affect who we're becoming as individuals?
- How can my loved one and I communicate better?
- How are we going to fight when it comes to that?
- How do we find healing for deep-seated issues?
- What should our spiritual lives as individuals and as a couple look like?
- How can we build love for a lifetime?

I've grouped the challenges into three major themes that will be familiar to you if you've read *Relationship Goals:*

1. PURPOSE: what God is calling you to do with your life in this season.

2. HEALING: 'cause, bro, sis, you gotta deal with those issues you've got if you want to be released.

3. ONENESS: that loving unity that makes relationships, especially the marriage covenant, so strong.

You can't tell me that if you deal openly and honestly with all these topics, your relationship won't be changed by the end of the thirty days. It will!

Freedom is coming!

Love is gonna build!

Victory is on the way!

Say it with me: "Victory!"

Oops, sorry, I got excited and started preaching. But I hope you've got the idea of what a big deal this thirty-day challenge is going to be for your relationship.

I hope you and your boo will read these challenges and discuss them together. But even if your partner isn't interested in that, you as an individual can still read the book and the relationship will benefit.

Do you accept the challenge?

GO!

PURPOSE

We are God's masterpiece. He has created us anew in Christ Jesus, so we can do the good things he planned for us long ago.

—EPHESIANS 2:10

DAY 1   INVITE HIM IN

Look! I stand at the door and knock. If you hear
my voice and open the door, I will come in, and
we will share a meal together as friends.

—REVELATION 3:20

When it comes to the marriage relationship, I used to assume that two people who are each at about 50 percent come together and in combination make 100 percent (or as close to it as they can get). It even seemed biblical because we're told, "A man leaves his father and mother and is joined to his wife, and the two are united into one" (Genesis 2:24). In other words, I thought the marriage equation was ½ + ½ = 1. In my mind, that was why people call their spouses "my other half" and say things like "You complete me."

Jerry Maguire is such a liar.

I've been married for over a decade now, but I realized early on that my original marriage equation was all wrong. The equation for marriage is really this: 1 + 1 + 1 = 1.

Are you currently questioning everything you learned in second-grade math class? Let me help you. One whole man plus one whole woman plus God in their midst creates one healthy marriage.

If you're dating seriously or engaged, God should be in the middle of that relationship too. What's different is that you don't have a marriage covenant together. But God still wants to be the center and the source of unity for the two of you. If you're headed for marriage, know that you're supposed to be entering into a 1 + 1 + 1 relationship.

No matter what your official relationship status (married, engaged, dating, it's complicated), it's important for the health of the relationship that you've been working on yourself, trying to make yourself the best you that you can be. Hopefully your partner has been doing the same. But even more important is the presence of the Third Member in the relationship. God's participation makes it possible for the man to fulfill his purposes, for the woman to fulfill her purposes, and for the relationship to fulfill its purposes.

Let's go back to marriage because I want to create a visual in your mind.

A godly marriage is like a triangle. First, the husband and wife are connected at the bottom of the triangle. When this is done in marriage, this is a beautiful connection, an honored connection, one that is intended to bring life to both people. From day one of their marriage, a wife and husband are bound together in a holy covenant. The bond is intended to last for a lifetime, and they will hopefully be strengthening their connection and enjoying the rewards of it for as long as they live.

But there's another part of the triangle. God is at the top, with each of the marriage partners spiritually connected to Him (assuming they're both believers in Jesus). This gives them another way to be connected—through God. And look at this: it's a geometric and spiritual truth that as each partner draws closer to God, each one is also drawing closer to the other. The fact that God is in the middle of that marriage is the key to their getting the relationship win.

GOD SHOULD BE IN THE MIDDLE OF *ANY* GODLY RELATIONSHIP.

Again, God should be in the middle of *any* godly relationship. When you're going out or chillin' at home with your bf/gf, God is on the date too. If you're in that engagement period where you're working on merging two lives into one, God is watching to see how you prepare for the marriage triangle.

Now, this triangle thing is probably not an entirely new idea to you, especially if you've read *Relationship Goals*. But let me ask you something: Have you two, as a couple, ever actually invited God into the midst of the relationship? Maybe it hasn't occurred to you to do that. Or maybe you've just assumed He would automatically be there so you didn't need to pay any attention to Him.

Or maybe once (like at your wedding) you *did* consciously ask God to be at the center of your relationship, but since then you've mostly forgotten about it.

If you've been more or less ignoring God's role in your relationship lately, then I can assure you that the persistent knocking sound you hear is Jesus at the door of your hearts, telling you He wants to come in. All you've got to do is turn the knob and say, "Hey there, Lord! C'mon in!"

My wife, Natalie, and I have found that there's a big value in consciously committing or recommitting a rela-

> THE PERSISTENT KNOCKING SOUND YOU HEAR IS JESUS AT THE DOOR OF YOUR HEARTS, TELLING YOU HE WANTS TO COME IN.

tionship to Christ's lordship. Today could be the day when you drive a stake into the spiritual ground and, together, ask God to be the leading figure, the guide, and the unifying power in your relationship. (When I talked in the introduction about taking action to solidify gains and prevent relationships from slipping back to the way they were before, this was just the kind of thing I was talking about.)

So here's your first—and most important—challenge: invite God into your relationship. This might just give you a change in perspective that helps you see your relationship in a whole new way from here on out.

DISCUSS

- What areas of your relationship have you been keeping God out of? And why have you been doing that?
- Are you prepared for changes that might have to happen when God takes His rightful place at the center of your relationship? Why or why not?

Spend time in prayer together with your significant other, inviting God to take control of your relationship and to guide and bless you in it.

NOTES ON ISSUES WE DISCUSSED, PLANS WE MADE,
AND THINGS WE BELIEVE GOD IS SAYING TO US:

DAY 2   THIRSTY FOR GOD

O God, you are my God;
   I earnestly search for you.
My soul thirsts for you;
   my whole body longs for you
in this parched and weary land
   where there is no water.

—PSALM 63:1

When you're trying to decide what movie to see on date night or how to load the dishwasher or whatever, you might not be thinking too much about your *purpose*. But I've got news for you—good news. God's had a purpose for you since before you were born.

Does that mean God has a purpose in what you do on a Friday night or in how you clean the kitchen? Yes, in a way. When we have a clear target for our purpose as individuals and our purpose as a dating or married couple, it affects everything we do.

Paul the apostle told us, "We are God's masterpiece. He has created us anew in Christ Jesus, so we can do the good things he planned for us long ago" (Ephesians 2:10).

So, first of all, let me tell it to you straight: if you're dating someone and what you're doing together or talking about or dreaming about wouldn't fall in the category of "good things," you need to reevaluate your activities. In fact, if your significant other isn't a part of your doing anything significant, it might be time to move on. (See chapter 5, "Does It Need to End?" in *Relationship Goals*.)

But what if you're in a more committed relationship? How can you look together toward the dreams God has for you? And here's the really amazing question: How can you as a couple live out God's purpose in even bigger ways than you could as individuals?

God doesn't leave us hanging when it comes to discovering His big ideas for our lives. Psalm 119:105 tells us that the Bible is "a lamp to guide my feet and a light for my path." God wants us to find Him. He wants us to know those good things He has in mind for us. After all, we can't hit our relational targets without knowing what they are.

So I'm telling you: Get into God's Word. Alone. Together. Online or audio or reading your granddaddy's leather Bible. Don't worry about how your mama or your best friend or the preacher down the street reads her Bible; just figure out something that works for you.

The important thing is that you're spending time getting to know God through His Word and prayer, because that's how you discover His purpose for you. Just like when you get to know someone new to your family. You spend time with him, you hear his stories, you learn what he likes and what he can't stand. The more you get to know him, the more you know automatically what's going to make him sad or mad or merry like Christmas. You learn the person's character.

IF GOD'S NOT ENOUGH FOR YOU, NO PERSON EVER WILL BE.

I can tell you right now that you will never know God completely. Why would we want to worship a God we could figure out? The more I know about God, the more I realize how much I have left to know. And that's okay with me.

The same thing goes for knowing our purpose. As we spend time with God, we get a better idea of His big plans for us. We see more clearly how our marriage or dating relationship fits into those plans. We see enough to get excited. We see enough to trash what isn't fitting with God's dreams. We see enough to want more.

I tell single people who are thirsty for a relationship, "Be thirsty for God. If God's not enough for you, no person ever will be." When you're in a relationship, you should stay thirsty for God.

So this week I challenge you to get into God's Word together. Of course, if you've just had a date or two, it might be too early for this. But if you're serious about each other, then going to Scripture together could be one of the best choices you make. Maybe you have your devotional times separately. Could you do that together? Maybe one person spends more time in prayer, Bible reading, and worship than the other. How could you both get more consistent in those things?

> **SEEKING GOD MAKES US THIRSTY FOR MORE. EACH TIME, WE FIND MORE OF HIM.**

Seeking God makes us thirsty for more. Each time, we find more of Him. And the better we know Him, the better we understand the purpose God has in mind for us.

DISCUSS

- What kind of devotional lives do the two of you already have?
- What might be some practical and helpful ways for y'all to seek God together?

∞

Make plans for (or reevaluate) devotional practices that you have with your loved one.

NOTES ON ISSUES WE DISCUSSED, PLANS WE MADE, AND THINGS WE BELIEVE GOD IS SAYING TO US:

DAY 3 YOU ARE WHO GOD SAYS YOU ARE

God said, "Let us make human beings in our
image, to be like us."

—GENESIS 1:26

Since we are his children, we are his heirs. In fact,
together with Christ we are heirs of God's glory.

—ROMANS 8:17

Whose image were you and your loved one made in? Kanye
and Kim? George and Amal? David and Victoria? No, God
made you to be like Him.

So if you or your loved one are letting your identity, your
character, or your personality be defined by anybody but
God, you are missing out on who you are supposed to be.
One of the best things the two of you can do to help each
other go from good to great is to get in the habit of reminding
each other of who you are in God.

Can I say something about this? The Enemy is going to
hate it. He's not scared of fakers and posers. He's scared of
people who find their purpose, know who they are, and don't
worry about what anybody else is doing but instead take their
stand and obey God.

Why do you wish you had a job like the one somebody else
has? Or a house like the one that other couple are living in?
Or the "perfect" family that you saw on Instagram? The

temptation to compare ourselves with others is always there because, if we give in, it gets us off our true identities.

There was this one preacher whose outfit I thought was cool. He was successful and where I thought I wanted to be, so I decided I should dress like him. I went to the store where this person got his clothes, and I put on the same stuff.

What I'd forgotten was that I've got thighs. And a booty. At the time, I had more of a gut. So when I looked in the mirror, trying to suck everything in, I just looked like a sausage. I felt like an idiot.

It's a good thing I've got Natalie. At times like this, she says, "Michael, you're comparing yourself with others. Don't forget who you are."

She's right. I can never be comfortable in the identity of somebody who's not me. I've got to be who God made *me* to be. And so does Natalie. And so do you and your bf/gf or h/w.

Here's a beautiful thing. None of us have to guess who we are. God's already given us our identities: we're the King's kids, made in His image and set up to rule. And if we're followers of Jesus, we're coheirs with Him of God's glory.

Don't you forget what the Word tells us, and don't let your loved one forget it either:

- Nothing is impossible for you because of Christ who lives in you!
- You are the head and not the tail!
- You are above only and not beneath!
- When you believe, mountains start to move!

Either you've accepted somebody else's identity or you know who you are in Christ.

The problem is that most believers have not been in the

Book enough to be able to find out their identities. So people on social media, in the neighborhood, or in business meetings tell us what our identity is, and we take on that perception.

God says, "Don't believe the lie. I created you the way you are on purpose. That little quirk? I'm going to use that to change people's lives. People are saying you're a burrito short of a combo? Don't worry about it. I want to use you to touch people who are missing some burritos."

> EITHER YOU'VE ACCEPTED SOMEBODY ELSE'S IDENTITY OR YOU KNOW WHO YOU ARE IN CHRIST.

Do you understand what I'm saying? God wants to use all of you. He wants to use all of your loved one too. But both of you have to know your identity is confirmed and affirmed in Him.

So, today I challenge you to assert your loved one's identity in Christ. For example, if your husband is feeling like his career is going nowhere, remind him that the Lord has created him with unique gifts and has a plan for him. Or if the mother of your babies is feeling like her life doesn't count because all she does is take care of ankle biters all day, remind her that God sees all she's doing and honors her.

How can you remind your loved one of his incredible God-given value?

DISCUSS

- What special qualities, gifts, and destiny do you feel that God has planted in your loved one?
- What things have perhaps been getting in the way of your loved one's living out his or her true identity?

∞

With love, and in godly confidence, affirm the identity that God has given your loved one.

NOTES ON ISSUES WE DISCUSSED, PLANS WE MADE, AND THINGS WE BELIEVE GOD IS SAYING TO US:

DAY 4   DON'T FULFILL YOUR POTENTIAL

May the God of peace—
  who brought up from the dead our Lord Jesus,
the great Shepherd of the sheep,
  and ratified an eternal covenant with his blood—
may he equip you with all you need
  for doing his will.

—HEBREWS 13:20-21

Why are you here on earth? What is that thing God has made
for you to do?

I hope you and your partner are getting clear on defining
each of your life purposes. I hope you understand that you
need a relationship that will help with those purposes, not
distract from them. But today I'm going to push you on something in this area. I'm going to try to clear up a common
confusion about purpose. Straighten this out in your minds,
and it might just be the missing piece that will explain why
your relationship hasn't been all it's supposed to be.

God has given us gifts and placed us in a world of opportunity. But that doesn't mean one choice about what to do
with our lives is as good as another. God has something specific He wants us to do, whether it's care for foster children,
start a business the world needs, write a book that will open
people's eyes, attack a certain type of injustice, or whatever.
That's why Hebrews says, "May he equip you with all you

JESUS NEVER REACHED HIS POTENTIAL. INSTEAD, JESUS FINISHED HIS CALLING.

need *for doing his will*" (emphasis added). We're given gifts and put on this world for a reason.

Are you ready to consider something mind blowing?

Jesus never reached His potential.

Instead, Jesus finished His calling.

When He climbed up on that cross and said "It is finished," everybody was like, "What is finished? Rome's still in power. Your disciples have all left you. This looks bad."

He wasn't finished with *what He could have done.*

He was finished with *what He was supposed to do.*

With His divine nature, He could have done anything. I mean, He could have become the richest man on earth, with everybody serving Him. He could have seated Himself on a throne in Jerusalem and been a more famous king than David. He could have gone to Rome and become Caesar.

But none of that was why the Father sent Him to earth. He came to shed His blood to seal an eternal covenant for sinners like you and me. For Him, that was doing God's will. That was living out His purpose.

The Enemy hates this. And so the Enemy tries to get us caught up in potential. Like many others have said, let me point out that the good is the worst enemy of the best.

You might think, *I can be a business owner. I can blog and vlog. I can run for mayor.* Maybe you could do all those things. But the question is, What is God calling you to do?

Let me tell you something: lots of people are busy and successful and yet die without ever reaching their purpose. We tend to think money, accolades, fame, or the ability to do something that nobody else can do is proof of fulfilling purpose. But that's really worldly success. And success and purpose aren't the same thing.

You can convince yourself and everybody around you that you're successful, but it's really because of something you contrived or something you were good at or something that just happened when you were in the right place at the right time. In that case, God could still be looking at you and saying, "You're completely out of what I called you to do."

This is why we have to divorce American culture and join with kingdom culture. Is that idea uncomfortable for you? Maybe you and your spouse or partner have been pursuing the American dream and doing a pretty good job of it. But remember what Jesus told the rich young ruler: "Go and sell all your possessions and give the money to the poor, and you will have treasure in heaven. Then come, follow me" (Mark 10:21). We never hear from this young man again because according to his culture, he had everything and he wasn't ready to give it up.

LOTS OF PEOPLE ARE BUSY AND SUCCESSFUL AND YET DIE WITHOUT EVER REACHING THEIR PURPOSE.

Jesus says to all of us, "Those who try to gain their own life will lose it; but those who lose their life for my sake will gain it" (Matthew 10:39, GNT).

What God's saying is "I want you to reach purpose, but I want you to do it in My will. I want to be in the center of your relationships, turning them into triangles. I want to be in the center of your life, guiding you. That's how to win."

So, does this cast a new light on what you and your loved

one are doing as individuals and as a couple? You wouldn't be the first if it does. It's not too late to change.

Don't fulfill your potential.

Fulfill God's specific will for your life.

DISCUSS

- How have the two of you been pursuing worldly success instead of godly calling?
- To the best of your knowledge, what is the specific calling of God on your lives?

Make a plan to change what you need to change in your lives and relationship if you are going to go all out in pursuing God's calling.

NOTES ON ISSUES WE DISCUSSED, PLANS WE MADE,
AND THINGS WE BELIEVE GOD IS SAYING TO US:

DAY 5   SAY YES

I heard the Lord asking, "Whom should I send as
a messenger to this people? Who will go for us?"
I said, "Here I am. Send me."

—ISAIAH 6:8

In yesterday's challenge we looked at how calling differs from
success. But now we need to move on to the leap-of-faith
part. Because, you see, you can't live out your purpose until
you say yes to God's calling.

Simple concept? Sure is. But I'll tell you, I was confused
about this for a long time. And I think a lot of other people
have a hard time with it too. If you and your significant other
want to walk out God's purposes for you as individuals and
as a couple, you'll have to learn to say yes to God.

Let me use myself as an example. I had a relationship with
God. I knew I had some gifts. But for years I didn't answer the
calling of God to use those gifts in the way God wanted me
to. So I wasted time doing stuff that wasn't bad but wasn't
exactly what God wanted me to do either.

I define a *calling* as "the intentional use of our God-given
gifts to influence the kingdom in a specific way." No matter
what realm God calls us to—government, education, sports,
entertainment, or whatever—we each have a calling to make
a kingdom impact with our gifts.

A lot of people are like, "Well, my gifts aren't in church."
They don't have to be. If you're in sales, kill that. If you're a

teacher, same thing. A coach, a trucker, a stay-at-home mom—doesn't matter. God has given you a calling to a purpose that impacts the kingdom.

Believers get messed up because once they find out what they can make money doing, they get used to doing it, they get known for doing it, and they just stay there. They never answer the call to go where they're really meant to be.

I've always been able to talk. I talked all the time. I talked so much that I got in trouble for it. But that was okay because I could talk my way out of the trouble. I could get people's attention by talking. I could persuade people by talking. My gift was talking.

With that gift, today I could be a radio host. I could be a sports announcer. I could read audiobooks for people. And maybe I would have been doing something like that. But God said, "I want to call you to speak to My people."

At that point, I had an option to say yes or no.

All of us get to that same point. The call can seem scary. It forces us to make changes. What are we going to do?

A lot of us start making excuses. Most believers, when it gets to right here, say, "God, I'm not ready for that." "God, I've not been trained for that." "God, it's too late for me."

GOD DOESN'T CALL PEOPLE WHO ARE EQUIPPED. HE EQUIPS PEOPLE WHO ANSWER THE CALL.

Moses said, "I don't talk well enough" (Exodus 4:10). (He had the opposite of my problem.)

Maybe God's called you to start a business. "Well, I didn't go to business school." He didn't ask you that! God's saying, "I did not ask you for your résumé. I asked you for your yes."

The beautiful thing about God is He

doesn't call people who are equipped. He equips people who answer the call.

If Abraham had said no to God's call to leave Ur, he wouldn't be the father of our faith. If Peter and Andrew had said no when Jesus asked them to follow Him, we would be missing these fishers of men and the rock of the church. If Isaiah hadn't said, "Here I am," somebody else would have had to go to the people of Israel.

We've got to say yes.

Yes.

Absolutely, Lord.

Here I am.

After you say yes, then God begins to mold you, remake you, change your desires, and take off the rough edges.

I hope you didn't see me when I was a youth pastor. I would cuss. I would say the N-word. Y'all, I was *rough*.

What God has done over time is put me on the potter's wheel. He has kept molding me, and so what you see now is because I said yes to a calling a long time ago. Where I'll be five months from now, five years from now, fifty years from now will be completely different because every day I wake up and say yes.

If you're going to reach your purpose, you have to say yes to the specific way God's going to use it to expand the kingdom. Not your kingdom. His kingdom.

You might need a push to do that. And that's one beautiful thing about a relationship with God at the center—you can push each other in a heavenly direction. Push each other to get past the inertia, past the excuses, past the fear. Push each other to say yes, and then say yes again and again every time God asks.

DISCUSS

- What fears or other obstacles are preventing you and your loved one from saying yes to God's calling?
- What are some things you've seen God do in the past that should give you confidence that He'll lead you safely today?

Encourage your partner to say yes to whatever God is calling him or her to do right now. Also, keep your partner accountable for follow-through.

NOTES ON ISSUES WE DISCUSSED, PLANS WE MADE, AND THINGS WE BELIEVE GOD IS SAYING TO US:

DAY 6 YOUR INNER CIRCLE

Don't go to war without wise guidance;
victory depends on having many advisers.

—PROVERBS 24:6

Who around you knows the real you? Not the Facebook you or the Instagram you or the enhanced you or the perfect-all-the-time you. I'm talking about the 4:00 a.m. you. The being-a-jerk you. The not-thinking-straight you.

Who knows what you struggle with? Who knows what your blind spots are and can see into those areas for you?

Who's in your life that has the Sit Down and Shut Up card? Who's got the guts to speak things into your life even when you don't want to hear it and you'll put up with it? Or whom in your life can you call when it's inconvenient for them and you know they'll put other things aside because they want to know about whatever big deal is going on in your life?

> WHO'S IN YOUR LIFE THAT HAS THE SIT DOWN AND SHUT UP CARD?

Who is that in your life?

I've asked these questions of many Christians, and honestly, most of them can't come up with names. Well, if they're married, they'll probably say their spouses. Other than that, nobody.

Of course it's good to be sharing things openly with your spouse, but that's not enough. Sometimes the issue in your life has to do with your partner. A married person needs somebody else—maybe another couple—to get raw and ugly with. Like, "I am mad at her. These are the reasons. Will you all pray for us? Now. Because I'm about to cut her and cuss her out."

Who's in your inner circle?

You might be thinking, *Pastor Mike, just chill on this. I got my clique. I got my dawgs. I got my girls. I got my besties. We tight. It's ride or die.*

But I'm not talking about people who have the same interests as you and are prepared to stick with you. I'm talking about people who will point you toward the interests of Christ.

See, we'll get it together with people around makeup, fashion, sports, TV, games, and whatever else we're into. There's nothing wrong with that. But when it comes to a moral compass, when it comes to our making the right decisions, when it comes to our deciding whether we're going to stay in a relationship, a lot of times people will give us advice based on their feelings and not based on their faith.

In a bad moment, you could say, "He broke up with me, Susie. We're going to slash his tires."

Susie ain't going to say, "Turn the other cheek." She's going to say, "Where's my knife?"

What I'm saying to you is this: because your friends will be down for wherever you are emotionally, that means sometimes they're down for delaying your purpose too. They'll let you stay in a relationship and never say anything to you when God showed them that was the wrong person.

We need honesty. Tough love. The Bible says, "Wounds from a sincere friend are better than many kisses from an enemy" (Proverbs 27:6). For some reason, as believers, we would rather get kisses from people who don't even know us than hear the hard truth about ourselves spoken to us in love.

But I'm convinced everybody needs a real inner circle. And by that I mean people who have the Holy Spirit in them, have some life wisdom built up, and want to see God's purpose achieved in our lives. Godly community, in other words. Everybody needs it.

> **BELIEVERS WOULD RATHER GET KISSES FROM PEOPLE WHO DON'T EVEN KNOW US THAN HEAR THE HARD TRUTH SPOKEN IN LOVE.**

Jesus chose godly community. He would literally walk past people and say, "Hey, follow Me! Walk with Me. Do life with Me." He picked twelve disciples, and out of them, He had three—Peter, James, and John—who He let even deeper into His life. These bros were His inner circle. They did everything together. They saw His most triumphant moments and His most vulnerable moments.

If Jesus needed an inner circle, doesn't it stand to reason we do too?

If two people are pursuing unity as a couple and purpose as individuals, they need godly community they can trust. As Proverbs 24:6 says, if we want to win in relationships, we've got to have advisers—the right kind of advisers—and listen to them. And both partners need to be comfortable about who is speaking into their lives.

Don't try to live life without godly community. Don't be haphazard one day longer about whom you will seek advice from when you need it. Get intentional about who is in your inner circle and who is out.

DISCUSS

- What was one time you got some really good advice? What was one time you got some really *bad* advice?
- Name the top five wisest people in your phone's contacts list.

Together with your partner, decide the people you will go to when you need godly advice that affects how you live out your purpose.

NOTES ON ISSUES WE DISCUSSED, PLANS WE MADE, AND THINGS WE BELIEVE GOD IS SAYING TO US:

DAY 7 SPEAK IT INTO BEING

Looking intently at Simon, Jesus said, "Your name
is Simon, son of John—but you will be called
Cephas" (which means "Peter").

—JOHN 1:42

When you live with somebody and see him every day, it's easy
to get used to *who he is* and forget about *who he is becoming*.
But the truth is, if we're in relationship with God through
Christ, He's got plans to mold us into something bigger and
greater. We all need to be reminded that we're in the process
of becoming, or else we can get stuck and discouraged.

A young man named Andrew started to follow Jesus. One
day he brought his brother, Simon, to meet Jesus. Then, as we
see in today's scripture, Jesus did something out of the
blue —He changed this guy's name from Simon to Cephas.

Let me help you understand this.

The name Simon has several meanings, one of which is "wavering one."
That's not very complimentary, is it?
Who wants a name that suggests he's
inconsistent and unreliable? But that
may have been just how this young
fisherman was.

Cephas means "rock" or "stone" in
Aramaic, the language that most people spoke in Israel at that time. It's the

> WE ALL NEED TO BE
> REMINDED THAT
> WE'RE IN THE
> PROCESS OF
> BECOMING, OR ELSE
> WE CAN GET STUCK
> AND DISCOURAGED.

same as Petros in Greek, which is Peter in English. These names all have the same meaning—"rock." Now, *there's* a name that's solid, tough, and dependable.

Remember, though, this was at the very beginning of Jesus's relationship with Peter, before Peter did anything impressive. At this point he was just a fisherman. But Jesus didn't want to address him as who he was; He wanted to address him as who he would be.

One of the best things we can do for people we're in godly relationship with is to keep their potential before our minds *and* theirs. That goes double when it comes to our significant others. Where our loved ones' character or spirituality or purpose is right now is not where it's going to be one day. And we need to speak to that, reminding our loved ones of where they're headed.

If your loved one shares a vision for the future, don't be like, "Oh, I don't know if that's going to work" or "I guess that's cool if that's what you want."

You should be saying, "Yeah, I see what you're talking about, and I know you can get there. I see God working. As a matter of fact, I'm going to fast and pray with you about this."

We shouldn't even wait for our loved ones to hint around for encouragement about their future identity. We should speak life to them whenever we can.

- "Maybe you're a little inconsistent now, but you are becoming a faithful man of God."
- "You're nervous about us becoming parents, but I can see that you're going to be a great mom."
- "God didn't put that creativity in you for no reason. He's going to use it."

- "I can't wait to see how God uses that teaching gift He's given you. The world needs your wisdom."
- "Keep going with med school because you're going to be an amazing doctor."

See, we serve a God who "calls into being things that were not" (Romans 4:17, NIV). He spoke the whole universe into existence. He's still creating something out of nothing in the lives of people who believe in His Son. And by faith, we participate in that creation.

Don't believe me? Well, what is the definition of *faith*? "Faith shows the reality of what we hope for; it is the evidence of things we cannot see" (Hebrews 11:1). It's almost like, in faith, something that hasn't happened yet already exists.

The confidence we show in our loved ones can actually be a part of what makes them into who God wants them to be. Faith changes things.

Long after Jesus changed Simon's name to Peter, this once-wavering fisherman was the first disciple to declare that Jesus was the Messiah. So Jesus reaffirmed his name change at that point. "I say to you that you are Peter (which means 'rock'), and upon this rock I will build my church, and all the powers of hell will not conquer it" (Matthew 16:18). The revelation Peter had received was going to be the stone foundation of Jesus's entire church. Peter was stepping into a place that had been only a possibility for him back at the beginning.

Don't you want to play a role in helping your partner go from potential to actuality in the plans of God? You can if you start today to create a habit of speaking to her in light of who she is becoming.

DISCUSS

- If you were going to give your loved one a name that represents where you think God is taking him or her, what would it be?
- How could it affect your relationship if both of you were getting regular encouragement about your future in Christ?

GO

Tell your loved one who you believe he or she can become through Christ. Make this a habit from now on.

NOTES ON ISSUES WE DISCUSSED, PLANS WE MADE, AND THINGS WE BELIEVE GOD IS SAYING TO US:

DAY 8 SINGLE IN A COUPLE

Carry each other's burdens.

—GALATIANS 6:2, NIV

Each one should carry their own load.

—GALATIANS 6:5, NIV

Aren't those two verses from Galatians interesting when you look at them side by side? Aren't they contradictory?

Not really.

Here's what I take away from this. In godly relationships, we're supposed to be helping each other. For sure. But at the same time, we also have to take responsibility for ourselves. Each of us reaps what we sow (Galatians 6:7). We'll all stand before the judgment seat of God as individuals someday, answering for our own choices (Romans 14:10, 12).

That's why I say in *Relationship Goals* that even when you're married, you should never stop being "single." What I'm talking about here is being an individual and pursuing the godly purpose and goals and interests you have for yourself, personally. As I said in Day 1, the marriage equation is 1 + 1 + 1—that is, a man, a woman, and God. Whether you're single, dating, engaged, married, divorced, or widowed, you've got to keep working on your own personal 1. That's your responsibility.

What's the point of finding a marriage partner who will support your purpose if you aren't going to go after it when you're married? Some people who are dating get too comfortable and stop thinking about their purpose, and the same thing can happen in marriage; it's a mistake either way. In a romantic relationship, you sacrifice your selfish desires for your partner, but you don't give up your God-given purpose. Keep that godly drive burning.

WHO ISN'T GOING TO GET BORED WITH A PARTNER WHO ISN'T GROWING OR DOING ANYTHING INTERESTING OR NEW?

And besides, who wants a relationship partner who sits on the couch watching TV whenever she has some spare time? Who isn't going to get bored with a partner who isn't growing or doing anything interesting or new?

So, let me ask you: What's the last thing you did to improve yourself? Here are some things you could be doing:

- Take an investment course, and create a plan to reach financial independence by a certain age.
- Set weight and physical fitness goals, and then work with a nutritional adviser, a fitness trainer, or whomever you need to reach those goals.
- Take a course online or at your local college to learn a foreign language, study art history, learn screenwriting, or study whatever else interests you.
- Plant a garden, and give away flowers to people who need cheering up.
- Go hiking or backpacking or mountain biking to renew your spirit in nature.
- Learn to cook. Stop feeding your family that nasty fast food!

Many people stop perfecting who God created them to be, just because they joined with somebody else. That's lazy. That's lack of vision. Don't you do that. Even though you're with somebody, keep working on your singleness—keep working on yourself.

Of course, you don't want to pursue self-enrichment *at the expense* of your relationship, especially if you're married. But don't *neglect* it either. This isn't selfish. When there's more to you—when you're more knowledgeable, more capable, more interesting, more experienced, more fulfilled—then you have more to offer to your relationship.

My first career was in music. I played drums and produced music. I worked with Universal Records and HBO and other clients. I loved it. But when God called me into ministry, I gave up my music.

But do you know what? I still have a passion for music. And I'm going back to developing and using those skills. Natalie supports me in this. It's fun for me, it's enriching for our marriage, and I think it will ultimately be of value to the kingdom of God as well.

What do you need to pursue to become a richer, more complete person? Nobody knows better than you. And nobody is more interested in learning about it than the one who loves you.

DISCUSS

- Confess ways you've gotten stuck in a rut.
- What topics or activities energize you?

Dream about ways you can develop the gifts and interests God has placed in you. Share these dreams with your partner, and write them in the notes space. Ask for your partner's support in your plans for personal growth.

NOTES ON ISSUES WE DISCUSSED, PLANS WE MADE, AND THINGS WE BELIEVE GOD IS SAYING TO US:

DAY 9 PERMISSION TO PURSUE

Trust in the LORD with all your heart;
> do not depend on your own understanding.
Seek his will in all you do,
> and he will show you which path to take.

—PROVERBS 3:5-6

How do you make decisions as a couple? What if one person is leaning one way while the other is leaning the opposite way? What if neither one of you has any idea what's best? What if you've lined up the pros and cons and the results seem to be pointing somewhere but you're still not feeling comfortable with the decision? What if the choice is causing you stress or creating conflict? What do you do then?

So many couples get bogged down or off track in their purpose right here. Let me see if I can help.

Natalie and I try to live our lives according to these verses from Proverbs. The lines are well known, but when we talk about relationships, they offer a new dimension.

"Do not depend on your own understanding." Does that approach sound familiar? Maybe you and your partner rely on reason, what makes sense logically, in making decisions. But I'll tell you what: We don't know all the facts. We don't know the future. So we can think we're doing the smart thing, but it's actually dumb. Many times, if we depend on our own understanding, we get ourselves in trouble.

For example, it might seem like the logical thing to accept a business opportunity that will give you more money. But what if that new position opens you to a level of greed that's going to corrupt your character? "More money—of course!" That's how the world reasons. God asks, "What will it profit a man if he gains the whole world, and loses his own soul?" (Mark 8:36, NKJV).

So, what are we supposed to do if we're not leaning on our own understanding? "Trust in the LORD with all your heart" (Proverbs 3:5). He knows it all. He's got the answer. He sees where the decision we're facing fits into His bigger plan. We don't have to heat up our brains trying to reason everything out and get all worried about making a mistake, but instead we should be trusting Him to lead us and work all things out for our good.

How do we do that? Well, look at the next verse. "Seek his will in all you do, and he will show you which path to take" (verse 6). Another translation says, "In all your ways acknowledge Him, and He shall direct your paths" (NKJV). That means that before we make a choice, we need to acknowledge God and ask Him, "Is this the path I'm supposed to take?"

I don't know about you, but I'm guilty of getting into things and then asking God to bless them afterward. It's so much better to pause, give God praise as the sovereign ruler over everything, and ask Him to give you insight. He'll let you know what you can go ahead with and what you shouldn't.

God gave me verbiage for this. He said, "Michael, I don't want you to do anything without permission to pursue." *Permission to pursue.*

I don't take a business deal anymore without permission to

pursue. I don't take an engagement to speak somewhere without permission to pursue. I don't get in relationship without permission to pursue.

When I acknowledge Him and am like, "God, hey. Am I supposed to get into business with them? Do I have permission to pursue?" He answers me yes or no. I'm not talking about an audible "Yes, son. You're supposed to pursue." But when I pray, I feel peace if it's the right thing to do or I feel a check if it's not the right thing to do.

The Bible tells us we see through a glass darkly. We're not going to get everything right. Sometimes I'm like, "God told me to do this," and then it pans out like "God was nowhere near that." But I've found that even if I make the wrong decision, God redeems the situation because I acknowledged Him.

Stay close to God, and work on perfecting your ability to understand what He's revealing to you. I've heard it said that God may show you the mountaintop and not the road in front of you or He may show you the road and not the mountaintop, but either way you've got enough to keep moving.

WHETHER GOD SHOWS YOU THE MOUNTAINTOP OR THE ROAD IN FRONT OF YOU, YOU'VE GOT ENOUGH TO KEEP MOVING.

So if you and your partner are facing a decision, go to God together and ask, "Do we have permission to pursue this?" A new job. A move. A different school for the kids. An investment. A summer mission trip opportunity. Whatever it is. Don't stress over it. Go to God. He knows everything, and He wants what's best for you.

DISCUSS

- What are some decisions you and your romantic partner are currently facing?
- How do these decisions fit with the godly purposes you've already identified for your lives?

Pray with your loved one, asking for God's guidance in one or more decisions you've got to make.

NOTES ON ISSUES WE DISCUSSED, PLANS WE MADE,
AND THINGS WE BELIEVE GOD IS SAYING TO US:

DAY 10   RE-PRESENTING CHRIST'S LOVE

> As the Scriptures say, "A man leaves his father
> and mother and is joined to his wife, and the two
> are united into one." This is a great mystery, but it
> is an illustration of the way Christ and the church
> are one.
>
> **—EPHESIANS 5:31–32**

We've got a one-word slogan that we use around our church.
It's all over our social media. I slip it into my messages. You
can find it printed on our church merch as a way of billboard-
ing our collective vision. What is that word?

Re-present.

It looks like it's only a single word, but we pronounce it
three ways:

- Pronounced reh-pree-ZENT (the usual way), it means
  we are living witnesses to God's grace. We represent
  God in the world.
- Pronounced ree-PREZ-cnt (as in, not the past or future
  but the *present*), it means we bring the gospel to the
  present, the way life today really is.
- Pronounced ree-pree-ZENT (like a speaker *presents*
  a message), it means a big part of our mission is
  to present Jesus's offer of mercy to people who need
  Him.

Dope, right? But what does this have to do with romantic relationships?

GOD'S PLAN OF ONENESS: ONE GOD, ONE MAN, ONE WOMAN, ONE MARRIAGE, ONE SEX PARTNER, ONE FLESH, ONE LIFETIME.

As I say in *Relationship Goals,* God's plan of oneness is for the closest human relationship to be one God, one man, one woman, one marriage, one sex partner, one flesh, one lifetime to create one picture. What I mean by "one picture" is the same thing Paul meant by "illustration" in Ephesians 5:32. The unity of marriage is the best way we have of getting an image in our minds of the unbreakable soul tie between Christ and His saved ones.

A lot of people out there in the world today say things like this: "I've never seen God. I can't believe in God." They need something to help them grasp what it's like to be in relationship with the invisible God.

I believe that was behind God's intention for marriage—that people who don't know Him would see a healthy marriage and would say, "Oh, I'm beginning to understand God's love for us now." And they would seek God at the same time they seek righteous relationships with other people.

Most of us can't afford to have an expensive painting, like one by Monet or Renoir or somebody like that. So companies make copies, or reproductions, of paintings like that for us. A lot of us, in our houses or apartments or dorm rooms, have a print like this on display. It's just a copy, but it's beautiful because it looks like the real thing and points back to the real thing.

That's what marriage is like. The real thing—the one-of-a-kind masterpiece—is God's relationship with His people. But a godly marriage is a beautiful copy we can all look at and admire. And what it reveals is an image of faithful, sacrificial love.

So, what I'm suggesting to you is a new way of looking at your marriage (or your future marriage, if you're still getting there). What if the marriage is not just you and your boo going about your days together? What if you took into account the spiritual message others might be getting when they look at your marriage? Maybe others could scope out the two of you and think, *Where does this kind of love and sacrifice come from?*

I hesitate to use the e-word because it throws so many people off, but could your marriage be a form of *evangelism*? As a married couple with God in your midst, you've got the power to reh pree ZENT, ree PREZ ent, and ree pree ZENT Jesus's love in a world whose #RelationshipGoals are so much shallower than what God offers.

Look, I'm not trying to put pressure on you, like, "Bro, sis, you'd better start faking a better marriage in public because other people's eternity could depend on it!" No. In fact, faking would be a good way to ruin the whole picture you're presenting. I'm saying that as you work on perfecting your unity, under the grace of God, there's an extra benefit you might not have taken into account: other people are watching and might be drawn toward God because of what they see.

When you're talking to others, be real about your marriage and about the place that faith has in your life. People will understand you're not perfect. But God will get the praise for the supernatural stuff that's going on inside that relationship. And other people—believers and not—will get a blessing from hearing about it.

DISCUSS

- Imagine that you're somebody else, looking at your relationship from the outside. How does the relationship reflect the love of Christ? How does it not?
- Evaluate your relationship in light of the three meanings of the word *re-present*.

GO

Talk with your spouse about how your relationship can be a better witness to others of Christ's love. If you make some new resolutions, be sure to write them down.

NOTES ON ISSUES WE DISCUSSED, PLANS WE MADE, AND THINGS WE BELIEVE GOD IS SAYING TO US:

HEALING

I am leaving you with a gift—peace of mind and heart. And the peace I give is a gift the world cannot give. So don't be troubled or afraid.

—JOHN 14:27

DAY 11 A WORLD OF TROUBLE

Here on earth you will have many trials and
sorrows. But take heart, because I have overcome
the world.

—JOHN 16:33

My wife and I have gone public with something since I
preached the original Relationship Goals sermons. I want to
share it with you now because I know that in some way you'll
be able to relate.

When our son, MJ, was almost two, we noticed that he
wasn't developing and talking and doing certain things like
Isabella, his older sister. So we took him to doctors and they
said, "Yeah, we think he has some developmental delays."

My wife, Natalie, and I were like, "No. Not our son. We've
prayed. We've fasted. We've cried. We've dedicated him to the
Lord. Not happening."

So we took him to other therapists, knowing that God is
bigger, knowing that we trust Him, and they said, "We're not
sure about it. He's not old enough to tell yet. But he looks like
he might have signs of autism."

Natalie and I went through a season of mourning when we
heard that. We're still in that season, in fact, even though we
believe and trust in God's faithfulness. I'm asking, "God,
what are You doing? I serve Your people. I do all this stuff for
You and Your kingdom. How does all this make sense?"

And God says, "Son, it's not something I'm doing *to* you. It's something I'm doing *for* you. I'm using your son, who carries your same name, to teach you about My faithfulness, to teach you about My grace. That's not going to come from photos you post on Instagram because he's cute. It's going to come from inside you and MJ and Natalie. It's going to come from you being connected to Me. It's going to come from you trusting that I've got it."

And all I can do is respond, "I trust You."

Then God took me to a scripture that has helped me through many days. "Dear brothers and sisters, when troubles of any kind come your way, consider it an opportunity for great joy" (James 1:2). I had never looked at that scripture with much faith because nothing had happened to me that hit me to my core like this. But now God was saying to me, "Michael, don't worry. When troubles of any kind come your way, I want you to change your perspective, and I want you to consider it an opportunity for your joy to grow, for your character to grow, for fruit to come out of this. Mike, it's going to be okay. For you know that when your faith is tested, your endurance has the chance to get stronger. So let it grow. Don't fight it. Don't deny it."

The Enemy tried to get me not to share anything about this so people wouldn't label my son. But God said, "I'm going to get the glory out of this. I'm going to do a miracle behind this. I'm going to be the One who is high and lifted up, and I'm going to be the One to get the glory."

I hope you and your loved one are deliriously happy together. But I know that sooner or later—this world being what it is—you will have suffering. Illness. Conflict. Unfulfilled dreams. Scarcity. Loss.

In fact, I'm sure you've already had hurts in your life. Quite possibly, worse ones than I've experienced. They're affecting your purpose and your relationships.

But I can say to you confidently, on the basis of the Word of God and my own experience, that when we hope in God instead of in our circumstances, we won't be disappointed. We won't need anything else.

> **WHEN WE HOPE IN GOD INSTEAD OF IN OUR CIRCUMSTANCES, WE WON'T BE DISAPPOINTED.**

To this day, MJ has never spoken a word. I'd give anything to hear my son speak. You wouldn't have to give me no more clothes. I wouldn't have to drive a car or own a house. But God says, "When I work this miracle in your behalf, you're going to see that the things you think are really important are not important at all."

God can bring healing to our hearts and spirits. And as He's doing it, He does some painful but necessary work of shaping us into the people He wants us to be. The relationships He's given us are a safe place of love and connection where this work can take place.

Jesus says to you, "Take heart, because I have overcome the world."

In the next challenge we'll look specifically at the problems that happen to relationships.

DISCUSS

- What are the toughest things you and your romantic partner are going through right now?
- How do they affect your faith and other parts of your lives?

∞

Identify ways that God is calling you and your partner to trust in Him in the midst of your struggles. Write them down.

NOTES ON ISSUES WE DISCUSSED, PLANS WE MADE,
AND THINGS WE BELIEVE GOD IS SAYING TO US:

DAY 12 HOPE FOR YOUR HURDLES

Get wisdom; develop good judgment.
Don't forget my words or turn away from them.

—PROVERBS 4:5

If you look up #RelationshipGoals, one thing I don't believe you'll ever find is people who look like they have problems. The couples who show up on Instagram look perfect. They never argue. They don't misunderstand each other. They couldn't possibly get grossed out by each other's smell. They've arrived.

And that's how you know the images are fake.

Real relationships have problems. Everybody is going through something in relationship that is a hurdle. Maybe you have a communication problem—you're trying to talk things out with your partner, but somehow it comes out as anger. Or the little annoyances and differences that were no big deal early in your relationship seem to have built up to a point where they're unbearable, and you don't know what to do about it. Or money is so scarce that both of you are scared and you fight over what to do with the little money you have.

> REAL RELATION-SHIPS HAVE PROBLEMS.

In *Relationship Goals*, I told the story of how Natalie's and my unfaithfulness to each other when we were dating led to problems we had to work through after we were married. Ten months of insanity led to ten years of insecurity. Because of what happened, neither of us was quite sure we could trust the other one. Even after years of marriage, Natalie would be watching the sisters I hugged at church. And I would remind her of what she'd done wrong. Actually, both of us were faithful to each other in marriage, but we still had these suspicions. It was horrible.

God has finally healed us of all that doubt and mistrust. But the point is, it was a process. Other people, looking at us, wouldn't have known what we were dealing with in our relationship.

There are other stresses in our life too. We have three kids, and as I told you yesterday, one of them has severe special needs. Do you think that isn't hard on our marriage? Our lives are really busy with growing ministries. We have the same discussions other couples do about who is the most tired and who is going to do what work around the house.

It's a process. We're learning and growing. Like Proverbs says, wisdom is something that develops over time.

LET'S STOP ACTING LIKE WE'VE GOT IT ALL TOGETHER, AND LET'S NOT EXPECT EACH OTHER TO HAVE IT ALL TOGETHER EITHER.

Our church has a saying: *progression, not perfection.* Let's stop acting like we've got it all together, and let's not expect each other to have it all together either. Enjoy the good times in your relationship, but don't despair when there are hard times too. Just keep working at it.

Philippians 2:12–13 says, "Work hard to show the results of your salvation, obeying God with deep reverence and fear. For God is working in you, giving you the desire and the power to do what pleases him." We work and God works in us.

One big help for you in all this is other couples who are prepared to be honest about their struggles. Revelation 12:11 talks about people who defeated the Enemy "by the blood of the Lamb and by their testimony." Did you catch it? *Their testimony.* Look, it's powerful when we open up about both our hardships and the grace we see within them.

Tell your story so that others can see how you're struggling. Listen to other people who have similar problems. Learn from one another about how God is helping.

Since our son, MJ, was diagnosed with autism, we have talked with many other parents who have kids with special needs. What we've learned is that the sadness we feel about our son's condition is normal. And the stress it puts on our marriage is normal too. But it's encouraging to know that others are making their way through it.

Whatever hurdles are between where you are now and where you want to be, remember this: you are not alone, and there's hope for the future.

DISCUSS

- What is discouraging you?
- Think of someone you know who has gone through what you're going through. What can you learn from him or her?

Give your loved one realistic yet faithful encouragement in an area that you know is hard for him or her now. Write it down so that your partner can come back to this page and reread it at any point.

NOTES ON ISSUES WE DISCUSSED, PLANS WE MADE, AND THINGS WE BELIEVE GOD IS SAYING TO US:

DAY 13　DOUBT INTERVENTION

Peter went over the side of the boat and walked
on the water toward Jesus. But when he saw the
strong wind and the waves, he was terrified and
began to sink. "Save me, Lord!" he shouted.
　　Jesus immediately reached out and grabbed
him.

—MATTHEW 14:29–31

Today's scripture is part of a familiar story where the disciples
were in a boat and Jesus appeared to them, walking on the
water. We're going to move through this story quickly, and
I'm going to encourage you to be like Jesus in four ways when
it comes to the faith of your loved one.

First, in this Bible story, the disciples were like, "Is that
Jesus out there? Nah, bro, couldn't be."

Peter said, "Lord, if that's You, tell me to come on out to
You on that water."

Jesus said, "Come on, then."

Here's the first thing you can do for your partner if you
want him to be a person of faith. *Call out faith.* If you really
believe it's a part of your loved one's purpose to do something, push him.

"You've been wanting to start that business for six years
now, but you're gun-shy. It's time to do it. I'm okay with you
committing our savings to this thing."

"You've been just fooling around with writing songs. But
you know what? They're really good. If you don't write them,

the world will never hear them. So, don't you think you should take this seriously and go after it?"

Second, when Jesus called him, Peter got the courage to step out of the boat. The other disciples were like, "Bro, this is crazy. He's about to drown. He can't even swim." But that man started defying the laws of physics.

Then he looked at the waves and the wind. When he took his eyes off Jesus, he started to sink.

What do we tend to do when somebody else tries something and it goes south? Sometimes we're tempted to blame. "I told you so." "She should have listened."

But what did Jesus do? He reached out and grabbed Peter's arm and pulled him up.

So, if you care about your partner's life of faith, the second thing you can do is *help her when things go wrong.*

Maybe your spouse wanted to move into a big, expensive house. You didn't think the two of you were financially ready for that, but you went along with it. Now your partner's income dropped and you can't afford the mortgage. Say, "It's okay. We can downsize. We're in this together, and I love you too much not to help in this situation."

Third, Jesus reached out to hold on to Peter, but He also got honest with him. "You don't got no faith, boy. Why'd you doubt?"

If you care about your loved one, the third thing you need to do is *confront his unbelief.* Times of doubt might be natural, but we're supposed to live a *super*natural life. Unbelief is not where we're supposed to stay.

What do you say if your partner is struggling with trusting God? "Come on, now. Don't you get into this pattern of doubt. Remember how we've seen God act for us before. He never promised to explain everything or give us an easy road all the time, but that doesn't mean He's not here and He's not real. Let's get back to praying and praising Him and trusting Him to act."

Fourth, Jesus didn't leave Peter floundering in the waves. They climbed back into the boat together, and the wind stopped. Or, in other words, the thing that distracted Peter went away when they both got back to a place where they could regroup together.

> THE THING DISTRACTING PETER WENT AWAY WHEN HE AND JESUS GOT BACK TO A PLACE WHERE THEY COULD REGROUP TOGETHER.

When the winds of life come and your partner is drowning in unbelief, the fourth thing you need to do is *be there with her.* Pick her up. Help her reset. Don't give up on the relationship.

Going through a faith struggle can be the thing God uses to make you both stronger in your purpose as a couple.

DISCUSS

- What is challenging your faith right now?
- How is the doubt affecting you?

If your partner is struggling with doubt, give support and encouragement to turn to God.

NOTES ON ISSUES WE DISCUSSED, PLANS WE MADE,
AND THINGS WE BELIEVE GOD IS SAYING TO US:

DAY 14 HERE'S MUD IN YOUR EYE

[Jesus] spit on the ground, made mud with the saliva, and spread the mud over the blind man's eyes. He told him, "Go wash yourself in the pool of Siloam" (Siloam means "sent"). So the man went and washed and came back seeing!

—JOHN 9:6-7

Today let's start with the Bible story, and afterward I'll connect it with your relationship.

In John 9 we read that Jesus and the disciples were walking along one day when they met a blind man. Jesus spit on some dirt to make mud and put it on his eyes. And the man was instantly healed! Wrong. Actually, he was still blind at this point.

There was something else he had to do before he got his miracle. Jesus told the man to go wash off the mud in a nearby pool of water.

Now, have you ever thought of this? That man had to walk to the pool blind and with mud in his eyes. I'm picturing him going step by step, very carefully, to find his way to the pool of Siloam. It was only later—after he got to the pool and washed—that his vision appeared.

Now, here's the lesson:

If you've prayed and you've trusted that Jesus will do some miraculous work in your relationship, you might have to be

IF YOU'VE TRUSTED JESUS TO DO MIRACULOUS WORK IN YOUR RELATIONSHIP, BE PATIENT AND KEEP THE FAITH THAT IT WILL COME IN TIME.

patient and keep the faith that it will come in time, not necessarily immediately.

There are still going to be moments of tension.

"Why ain't you taking the trash out?"

"Why didn't you pay the bills?"

"Why did you tell the kids they could have ice cream? I already told them they needed to go to sleep."

I don't know what your issues are. They might go a lot deeper than just getting annoyed with each other. But whatever they are, real life with two imperfect people trying to live together in an imperfect world will happen.

The Bible says that two are better than one. At everything. Even at messing up. But that doesn't mean God isn't at work. And we have our part in that.

The man in John 9 had to walk without seeing to the pool of Siloam. The miracle had already started—he had the mud in his eyes as proof. But he had to go step by step before he saw the miracle completed.

Jesus could have been like, "Hey, bro, take My hand. Let Me walk you to the pool."

But no. What He said was, "I'm going to stay here, and I'm going to see if you obey the last instruction I gave you. Walk to the place where you can wash. And if you obey what I'm telling you to do, you'll be able to see a miracle."

How is God expecting you and your loved one to obey Him? What do you need to do, step by step, to see God create positive change in your relationship? Is it going to counseling week after week? Is it talking things out, admitting wrong and forgiving? Is it finding a couple to mentor you? What is it?

The blind man met Jesus, but he would not have been able to see if he had not followed Jesus's full instructions. You, too, need to do your part in seeing the transformation God is bringing about. It might not look pretty. It might look like somebody with mud smeared on his eyes. But it's all part of the process. Remember from Day 12—progression, not perfection.

I love that Siloam means "sent," because this man was sent there to bring his healing to conclusion. Godly couples are also sent on a journey—not an easy one—of becoming who God has purposed them to be.

God is saying to you, "I knew you before you were formed in your mother's womb. I've commissioned you. I have a plan for you. I have a plan for your relationship. What I put together, let nobody and nothing take apart."

He'll do His part. You do your part too.

DISCUSS

- Where do you need to see a miracle in your lives or relationship?
- What has waiting for this miracle felt like?

If you and your loved one can agree on what God is calling you to do to prepare for a miracle in your relationship, make a plan for being faithful to do it. Record your plan on the next page.

NOTES ON ISSUES WE DISCUSSED, PLANS WE MADE,
AND THINGS WE BELIEVE GOD IS SAYING TO US:

DAY 15   DAMAGED GOODS

The LORD says, "I will give you back what you lost
to the swarming locusts, the hopping locusts,
the stripping locusts, and the cutting locusts."

—JOEL 2:25

If your relationship is like most, then I can tell you that a lot of the problems you're going through as a couple don't come from the relationship itself but from previous relationships. They come from relationships with your family of origin, friends, teachers, coaches, bosses, and former lovers—people like that. None of us had the luxury of being surrounded in a perfect environment. We're all damaged goods.

Like, maybe your perception is damaged. You're a glass-half-empty kind of person. If something good is coming your way, you're always like, "What's the catch?" It causes you to be mistrustful of your partner and other people in your life. But where did this thing come from? Well, maybe you had a divorced father who would tell you he would pick you up on Friday but he never came. You got damaged. You still have the perception that good things will never come to pass.

A conflict arises and you get angry—way angrier than the situation deserves. Your anger gets in the way of constructive solutions and reconciliation. Your significant other might even be scared of you. But your anger is not just your anger. You learned that response because you grew up in an angry household.

> A LOT OF THE PROBLEMS YOU'RE GOING THROUGH DON'T COME FROM THE RELATIONSHIP ITSELF BUT FROM PREVIOUS RELATIONSHIPS.

I told in *Relationship Goals* about how I struggled with sexual sin. I also wrestled with lust and a pornography addiction. One time, after I'd already been in some wrong relationships and had sex before marriage, I went to New York with my dad. While we were there, he told me a story I'd never heard before.

"Son, I went on a trip to New York with the Grambling State men." He used to be on the football team when he was at that university. "I was a young man and I was still a virgin, but I had these images and thoughts in my head. Back then, they had what you called peep shows, down in Times Square. You walked down this street, and if you put a quarter in, then the blinds would go back and you would get to see a naked woman." He said, "Son, I walked down that street with a pocketful of quarters."

My dad had struggled with the same kind of problem I did. I dealt with the upgraded version—internet porn. But my point is, he had this same tendency toward sexual sin, he gave in to it, and he never prepared me for dealing with it.

Now, my dad is a great man. He's my hero. But even the best parents and aunties and uncles and grandparents are going to fail us or injure us somewhere along the way without intending to.

And the reason our early damage continues to harm us is that the Enemy won't ever let us forget it. Did you know the devil has a goal for his relationship with you? His relationship goal is to steal, kill, and destroy (John 10:10). He whispers, "You're nobody. You're nothing. You'll never be what God intended."

Maybe you've been listening to those whispers. Maybe you think you've wasted too much time. Even if you could heal the damage from early in your life, you figure it's too late to change your relationship. It's too late to restore your purpose. Too late to be victorious in Christ in this world.

The prophet Joel talks about a harvest destroyed by a locust plague. The people went through a hard time. But then another year came around, and it was a different story.

> The rain he sends demonstrates his faithfulness.
>> Once more the autumn rains will come,
>> as well as the rains of spring.
> The threshing floors will again be piled high with grain,
>> and the presses will overflow with new wine and olive
>> oil. (2:23–24)

God can restore what's been lost to you and give you even more.

If your relationship is in trouble—maybe hanging on by a thread—because of something in you, get at the core issue and work on it. Talk with your partner, a sibling, a mentor, a counselor, or somebody else who can help you figure out where the problem originated. Because you need to identify what your damaged area really is before it can be healed.

DISCUSS

- What are the top areas you feel you need healing in, and where did they originate?
- What lies surround these issues?

GO

If you've been letting an emotional wound fester, identify something you can do to begin or speed up the healing process. It will help you and your relationship!

NOTES ON ISSUES WE DISCUSSED, PLANS WE MADE, AND THINGS WE BELIEVE GOD IS SAYING TO US:

DAY 16 GO TO THE MANUFACTURER

Search me, O God, and know my heart;
test me and know my anxious thoughts.
Point out anything in me that offends you,
and lead me along the path of everlasting life.

—PSALM 139:23-24

Here's a problem I see in lots of romantic relationships: One of the partners will expect his significant other to complete him or fix him or make him whole. A lot of people are basically holding their wives or husbands, or their boyfriends or girlfriends, hostage to fix a problem they didn't create. The problem comes from before the relationship even started, probably back to their families of origin, like we saw in the previous challenge.

There's an anger problem. There's a lust problem. There's a commitment problem. There are bad habits of laziness or put-downs or lack of confidence. Whatever it is. Sure, it's good for people to recognize they're dealing with a problem like this, but they've also got to deal with it in a way that's helpful to them and their relationship, not making things worse.

> A LOT OF PEOPLE ARE BASICALLY HOLDING THEIR SIGNIFICANT OTHERS HOSTAGE TO FIX A PROBLEM THEY DIDN'T CREATE.

What does it do to a relationship when one person expects the other one to fix her? It creates unfair pressure. It produces resentment. It gets in the way of oneness. Look, relationships are hard enough without all this nonsense. Don't you agree?

So, what do you do if you recognize you've got a long-standing problem and you want to finally take care of it? Well, what if you buy a product and it has a defect? Probably you take it back to the manufacturer because the manufacturer knows all about it. Same thing if you need repairs in your emotions or your spirit—you go to your Manufacturer, your Creator.

Maybe you've got today's psalm in mind and you think you're ahead of me and you're saying right now, "Ain't nothing wrong with me, Pastor Mike. I'm beautifully and wonderfully made."

Okay. You *are* beautifully and wonderfully made. The Creator doesn't make any mistakes. There are no manufacturer defects with us. But there's also such a thing as sin. And it affects all of us from the day we were born. It takes that beautiful design God has for us and scribbles graffiti all over it.

What we see from this psalm is that when we get messed up, we have to go to our Creator for fixing. Why? Because only He truly knows us. He's not fooled by how you act when you're out in public or what you post on Instagram. He knows you for real, inside and out, even more than your relationship partner ever will.

So, get this straight: Your significant other can't fix you. Only God can. Because He knows you.

David was able to pin this in such an amazing way in Psalm 139. Let's look at more of it.

> O Lord, you have examined my heart
>   and know everything about me.
> You know when I sit down or stand up.

You know my thoughts even when I'm far away.
(verses 1–2)

Key words here? *Far away.*

Your relationship with God might look a lot different from what it should. You may not be close to God. You may not believe at all. But I want you to know that your Creator still knows your thoughts and He knows you, even if you're far away.

And this is the thing about God: He doesn't want to be apart from you. He wants to be connected to you. So no matter what the condition of your relationship with God is, it's still true that He's the one you need to go to for fixing. Maybe He'll heal you *and* draw you closer to Him.

Now, watch how powerful this next statement is:

I could ask the darkness to hide me
and the light around me to become night—
but even in darkness I cannot hide from you.
To you the night shines as bright as day.
Darkness and light are the same to you. (verses 11–12)

Key word? *Darkness.*

I don't care how dark your situation is right now, how bleak it looks, how relationally deprived you are, how damaged, how addicted. Even in your darkness, you cannot hide from God. He sees you. He knows you. He loves you.

Some people will give up before they even approach God for help. Why? Because they think it's hopeless. Even God can't help, they think.

No, no, no. What seems like night to you is bright as day to God. Your problem might be big and nasty, and it might have been there for a really long time, but it's still well within God's ability to deal with. Don't let the darkness intimidate you. Let God shine His light on your situation.

God's Word has the truth to correct the falsehood you've listened to. His Spirit is the comforter who comes alongside you. His church is a community that gives you a place of belonging. He has gifted pastors, teachers, and others who can speak into your life. His method of discipleship forms us into true followers of Jesus. His forgiveness washes away guilt totally and forever. His patience is great. His wisdom is perfect. He's always ready to listen. He's got peace for us so extreme it doesn't even make sense. He's got it, my friend.

So please, please, take the pressure off your loved one. Go to the Maker who knows all your design specs. He will bring healing and lead you along the path of everlasting life.

DISCUSS

- How have you been putting unfair expectations on your partner to heal you?
- How have you been underestimating God's ability to fix what's wrong with you?

G⊖

If you've been expecting your loved one to do something for you that only God can do, apologize to your partner. And commit to seeking God for healing instead.

NOTES ON ISSUES WE DISCUSSED, PLANS WE MADE,
AND THINGS WE BELIEVE GOD IS SAYING TO US:

DAY 17   THE SECRET TO JOY

I have told you this so that my joy may be in you
and that your joy may be complete.

—JOHN 15:11, NIV

Many of us don't know where to get joy. We've misplaced it.
We get up, go to work or school, come home, do more work
or studying, go to bed. Maybe we have some happiness on a
Friday or Saturday night, but we rarely feel a deep-down joy,
even in our best relationships.

The thing is, joy is supposed to play a major part in our
lives. Take another look at the verse at the top of this page.
That's Jesus talking about the joy that comes from knowing
we're safe in His love. (Now might be a good time to pull out
your Bible and read all of John 15.)

This really is an anchor scripture for me. Even more, it's a
goal we each want to reach. And it's a goal Jesus wants for all
of us.

I can just picture the disciples He's talking to. They're like,
"He wants us to be filled with His joy." Then He emphati-
cally says, "Yes. But not only that. Your joy will *overflow.*"

I want you to realize that's what God wants for you individually and as a couple today. He wants joy to overflow in
your life. He wants you to be joyful or joy-full, full of joy.

But if we look at a lot of people's lives, they're not full of
joy. They're full of worry. They're full of doubt. They're full
of anxiety. If we believe in Jesus, how can we be dealing with

the same level of anxiety and pain and frustration as everybody else?

This is what God's saying: "I've got a key, but you're missing it. I've got something I want to give you. I don't want to give you happiness, because happiness is dictated by circumstances. I want to give you joy, which is something that only I can give, and it's something that starts from the inside."

See, happiness is one of those things that comes and goes. I mean, let's be honest. You wake up happy. Then you find out it's raining, and you have a bad day. You go to a restaurant, and they get your food order wrong. Y'all know, once they get my food order wrong, I'm tripping and it's a bad day. See, happiness goes up and down like a roller coaster. Joy is unmovable. Joy is an anchor. A lot of people try to find joy, but they look in the wrong places, so they settle for happiness.

Happiness is a feeling dictated by what is happening externally. But that's busted because I can never control that. I can't control whether my boss acts crazy. I can't control whether my car breaks down. I can't control whether I lose my job. So if I am happy based only on what happens on the outside, then I am never in control of my own life.

But joy is a posture of my heart that says two things: God's got it, and I trust Him, period. When I get fired from my job, God's got it, and I trust Him. When the economy is turned upside down and my children are acting crazy, I have a faith that stands and says, "God's got it, and I trust Him." When I've lost everything, I have to take a stance that God's got it and I trust Him.

> JOY IS A POSTURE OF MY HEART THAT SAYS TWO THINGS: GOD'S GOT IT, AND I TRUST HIM, PERIOD.

That kind of joy overflows into all our relationships and affects everyone around us, including our partners. That kind of joy helps us get through the hard times together because we know that God's got this and we can trust Him to help us through.

I don't know what the Enemy has been trying to tell you about your life, but I do know you have a lot to be joyful about. As you abide in Jesus and stay connected to Him, you will find joy no matter what's happening around you.

DISCUSS

- What's a hard thing that you and your partner are going through right now—something that's got you worried and on edge?
- How would you react to your circumstances differently if you really believed that God's got this?

Pray as a couple, asking God to build up the faith He's already given you. Thank Him for the joy that comes from being in Jesus.

NOTES ON ISSUES WE DISCUSSED, PLANS WE MADE, AND THINGS WE BELIEVE GOD IS SAYING TO US:

DAY 18 SAYIN' IT SWEET LIKE HONEY

Kind words are like honey—
sweet to the soul and healthy for the body.

—PROVERBS 16:24

I made this claim in *Relationship Goals:* "Your words are either building up the person you want to be married to or they are tearing down the person you have to be married to." (Tricky, huh?) Think about that in relation to your partner.

What kind of person would you like him to become?

If you want him to be confident, are you expressing trust and encouragement? Or are you putting him down and pointing out every little mistake?

If you want her to feel secure in the relationship, are you reassuring her of your love? Or are you acting cold and distant with her so that she's wondering if she's really got your heart?

Seriously, think about it: through your speech and actions, you can actually help your mate become the kind of person you want to be with. What else is there that enables you to do that? This is better than plastic surgery!

Ephesians 4:29 gives helpful advice for romantic relationships: "Do not let any unwholesome talk come out of your mouths, but only what is helpful for building others up according to their needs" (NIV). The old King James Version uses a term here you've probably heard: *edifying.* It means the same thing. Build up. Don't tear down.

In counseling couples, Natalie and I have found that poor speech habits are a big issue in many troubled relationships. What's interesting is that a lot of people already realize they could do better in this area. They even realize it's important to do so. But still, for some reason they're reluctant.

Let me deal with some excuses *you* might have:

> YOUR WORDS ARE BUILDING UP THE PERSON YOU WANT TO BE MARRIED TO OR TEARING DOWN THE PERSON YOU HAVE TO BE MARRIED TO.

- "Edifying speech wasn't modeled for me when I was growing up." I get that. And sure, that makes it harder for you. But I don't care how old you are or how long you've been in a relationship—it's not too late to learn another way. Find people around you today who are good at giving their loved ones some honey with their words, and imitate them.
- "My partner doesn't build me up, so why should I do that for him?" I'll tell you what every mama has told every kid: two wrongs don't make a right. And your good example might be enough to change the rules of the game in the way you and your loved one speak to each other. I've seen it happen.
- "I know I'm more negative than I should be, but I've always been like that. I can't change now. It's a habit." Look, by the grace of God, I broke a porn addiction. By the grace of God, lots of other people I've known have broken bad habits like smoking, getting drunk, and overeating. You're going to tell me speech habits are tougher than that stuff? If you *want* to change in this area, you can. The Holy Spirit lives inside you and is your helper.

• Finally, "I'd feel awkward starting to talk sweetly this late in the game." This one's easy: *Get over it!* (You'll be glad you did, because you know we're talking about a win-win thing here, right?)

THERE IS POWER OF LIFE AND DEATH IN THE TONGUE. } There is power of life and death in the tongue (Proverbs 18:21). Give life to your loved one and give life to your relationship by speaking edification, kindness, encouragement, praise, compliments, interest, admiration, hope, faith, consolation, understanding, agreement, respect, gratitude, and all other good things. In other words, speak unto your loved one as you would have your loved one speak unto you. Can I get an amen?

Your words are either building up the person you want to be married to or they are tearing down the person you have to be married to. Choose well.

DISCUSS

• Listen to your partner tell how your speech could be more positive and elevating, and receive it humbly.
• Apologize as needed.

GO

Say nothing critical to your partner all day. Use edifying speech only. And let this day be a model for the future.

NOTES ON ISSUES WE DISCUSSED, PLANS WE MADE,
AND THINGS WE BELIEVE GOD IS SAYING TO US:

DAY 19 EPIC RECOVERY AFTER AN EPIC FAIL

Fear of the LORD teaches wisdom;
humility precedes honor.

—PROVERBS 15:33

In May 2014, our first child—Bella—was eight months old. Or to put that another way, this was going to be Natalie's first Mother's Day as a mother herself. It had crossed my mind that this was probably a big deal for Natalie. And come on, I'm a good husband, right? I intended to acknowledge the milestone appropriately.

I was about to get schooled.

The night before Mother's Day, Natalie and I took baby Bella and went to Target to get presents for our mothers. While we were browsing in the jewelry section, Nat pointed to a necklace, and she was like, "Ooh, this is nice."

I hadn't gotten around to buying Natalie a Mother's Day present yet, so I guess my Husband Holiday Hint Detector was turned on. Did she want this necklace? She'd pointed it out specially, it seemed to me. Target was her favorite store, so she must like the merchandise. Yeah, probably this was a clue for me.

While she wasn't looking, I went and bought the necklace. I might have even patted myself on the back about what a smart and caring husband I was.

The next day we woke up, and I gave the necklace to Natalie, eager to see her reaction.

She definitely reacted. She started crying. "This is it?" she said. "This is all you think of me, the mother of your child?"

You would have thought I'd given her a *disease* for Mother's Day! But the truth was, she was sad and hurt by my choice.

I was hurt too, at first, by her reaction. But then I thought about it. This present wasn't something I'd thought up on my own. I'd waited till the last minute to buy it. It didn't have any special meaning about Natalie or her motherhood. And (nothing against Target) the necklace was kind of cheap and ordinary.

This present had not been my best effort. I hadn't been as appreciative of Natalie's special day as I should have been. For real, this was husband-fail territory.

I got the message from this experience. Mother's Day might not be a big deal to me, and it might not be a big deal to some other moms, but it was *very* important to the mom I happened to be married to. It was maybe bigger than Christmas to her. So I made sure the next Mother's Day was special.

Nobody goes into a romantic relationship as an expert. None of us knows everything about our partner. We all have some false assumptions. We all make mistakes. The question is, Do we learn from our mistakes?

> **WE ALL MAKE MISTAKES. THE QUESTION IS, DO WE LEARN FROM OUR MISTAKES?**

If you make a mistake (and maybe your loved one makes it very clear that she doesn't appreciate it, like Natalie did with me), don't get discouraged. Don't give up on doing better. Become a student of your spouse and what pleases her—not just about gifts but also about communication; about how you use your time, money, and energy; about raising kids; and more.

Humility, godliness, and wisdom all go together. The Lord wants you to grow wise in relationships and every other area of your life. "If you need wisdom, ask our generous God, and he will give it to you" (James 1:5).

Increasing wisdom about your loved one should be one of those relationship goals you never quit on.

DISCUSS

- Ask your significant other about an area where you can improve in relating to him or her.
- Repeat the preceding question about a second area for improvement.

GO

Make a secret plan for surprising your loved one with a better outcome in an area where you've been falling short. Shh, don't tell! But *do* follow through!

NOTES ON ISSUES WE DISCUSSED, PLANS WE MADE,
AND THINGS WE BELIEVE GOD IS SAYING TO US:

DAY 20 PICKING UP AFTER YOU WERE LET DOWN

Make allowance for each other's faults, and
forgive anyone who offends you. Remember, the
Lord forgave you, so you must forgive others.

—COLOSSIANS 3:13

When you're in a romantic relationship with somebody, you think, *If there's one person I ought to be able to trust with my back, it's this person. If there's one person I can tell my junk to and be confident it's not gonna get spread around, it's this person. If there's one person I can rely on to do what she promised, here's that person.*

There's one problem with that: human nature.

Jesus should have been able to expect that Peter would stand by Him in His darkest days. In fact, Peter himself declared to the Lord, "Even if everyone else deserts you, I will never desert you" (Matthew 26:33). But then what happened? Within twenty-four hours, Peter denied knowing Jesus . . . three times!

How has your loved one lied to you, betrayed you, or let you down? Has he spent money after the two of you agreed to save it? Has she belittled you with her words, even though she promised she wouldn't do that again? Has he powered up on you in anger? Has she flirted with somebody else?

That kind of thing can get into your oneness and start making it feel more like twoness real quick.

I know you've heard all your life that you need to forgive.

I know you've listened to sermons on it, and I know you've read in the Bible the parable of the unforgiving servant and how we should forgive seventy times seven (Matthew 18:22). You know forgiveness is important. You have some experience with it.

But see, it's so easy to not *fully* forgive, especially when you're living in close relationship with somebody day after day after day. And any leftover bitterness and resentment can easily get in the way of your relationship goals as a couple. So what I'm asking today is that you take a survey of your heart to see if you have a leftover grudge in there or something you haven't been able to quite let go of.

> IT'S SO EASY TO NOT *FULLY* FORGIVE, ESPECIALLY WHEN YOU'RE LIVING IN CLOSE RELATIONSHIP WITH SOMEBODY DAY AFTER DAY.

Can I talk to husbands and wives? Some of you aren't seeing the change and the growth you want to see in your spouses because you will not let them be freed from what they used to be or allow them the grace to become new around you. That's why people get divorces and they see their exes five years later and they're like, "Why are they doing so good?" I would say to people like that, "Because they got away from *you*. Because in the midst of the relationship you couldn't let God work on your heart to be an extension of His love that He's been to you, so you're like the person who got ten million dollars of debt canceled but you're holding somebody hostage for ten cents."

Let that dime go!

After Jesus died, the disciples were out fishing, and someone came walking along the shore. One of them said, "Bros, that looks like Jesus."

Another one said, "There's no way that's Jesus. He died."

But it *was* Jesus. He made breakfast for the boys. And then something beautiful happened.

> After breakfast Jesus asked Simon Peter, "Simon son of John, do you love me more than these?"
>
> "Yes, Lord," Peter replied, "you know I love you."
>
> "Then feed my lambs," Jesus told him. (John 21:15)

They went through this same routine three times. Then Jesus said the same thing to Peter that He'd said to him at the beginning of their relationship: "Follow me" (verse 19).

Are you seeing how deep this is? Peter denied Jesus three times. Jesus gave Peter three chances to reaffirm his love. This right here was complete and thorough forgiveness of the offense. And then they started all over again in their relationship.

If we're guilty of something in a romantic relationship, we have to repent and be sorry about it, and the other person has to *know* that. Then the other person has to forgive us, and we have to *know* that he's forgiven us. And we both have to start over fresh and move on. Anything else will taint our love, break up our oneness, and delay our purpose.

Don't give up on your relationship because the other person has let you down. If Jesus, our example, had to forgive, don't you think we're going to have to do it?

DISCUSS

- What do you need to forgive?
- What do you need to have forgiven?

If you can do it sincerely, say the words "I forgive you." And let it go.

NOTES ON ISSUES WE DISCUSSED, PLANS WE MADE, AND THINGS WE BELIEVE GOD IS SAYING TO US:

ONENESS

Make every effort to keep yourselves united in the Spirit, binding yourselves together with peace.

—EPHESIANS 4:3

DAY 21   THE COMMUNITY AROUND THE COUPLE

All the believers devoted themselves to the
apostles' teaching, and to fellowship, and to
sharing in meals (including the Lord's Supper),
and to prayer.

—ACTS 2:42

We're moving on to the theme of oneness in relationship now.
Genuine, godly unity is a beautiful thing, and the fantasy land
of #RelationshipGoals has got nothing to beat it. But with
this theme, we're going to start in a place you might not expect. Because you see, a couple's Christlike oneness doesn't
exist all by itself; it exists inside the community Christ
created—the church.

I've got a radical idea for you: as
Christians, we'd have to do less evangelism if we did community better.
You wouldn't have to tell people
about Jesus because they would see
how you live your life and the people
you spend time with and they would
ask you, "What must I do to be saved?"

> WE'D HAVE TO DO
> LESS EVANGELISM IF
> WE DID COMMUNITY
> BETTER.

That's what happened to the early church that we read
about in Acts 2. In my Bible, the title above that passage is
"The Believers Form a Community." That's what I'm talking
about. As we see in today's scripture, the believers devoted
themselves to teaching, fellowship, meals, and prayer.

What happened next? "A deep sense of awe came over them all" (verse 43). And the apostles started performing miracles, signs, and wonders.

Awe. Wonder. Miracles. It all started in community.

But it gets even better: "All the believers met together in one place and shared everything they had. They sold their property and possessions and shared the money with those in need. They worshiped together at the Temple each day, met in homes for the Lord's Supper, and shared their meals with great joy and generosity—all the while praising God and enjoying the goodwill of all the people" (verses 44–47).

This community wasn't in competition with one another. They were *completing* one another. They were helping one another live out their individual purposes. And look at the result of their doing this: "Each day the Lord added to their fellowship those who were being saved" (verse 47).

How about you and your spouse or bf/gf? Unless your relationship is still in the getting-to-know-you stage, I've got a question for you: Are the two of you a part of a community where the Holy Spirit is alive and active?

Now, watching a livestream service or going to church every week and listening to a sermon is good, but *also* being in a small group or some other type of close Christian community is much better. Because that's where you get touched. Not just you individually, but you and your loved one together.

Take healing, for example.

Your pastor can't bring healing to all the people in your church who have emotional wounds. But if you're in a community, walking through life with others and asking them to pray for you, that's where healing comes. As God tells us in James, "Confess your sins to each other and pray for each other so that you may be healed. The earnest prayer of a righteous person has great power and produces wonderful results" (5:16).

Your relationship is broken? Get around some godly people. If your group keeps pointing one another to Jesus, praying together, and confessing together, healing will come.

Now, here's something about this that might sound controversial but shouldn't: if you're going to have godly community as a couple, you may have to divorce some of the friends you've had. I'm telling you, you can't stay in a friendship because of time served.

An old friend might have come to mind, and right now you might be thinking, *We've been down since second grade! We learned how to spell together.* Well, spell "Bye-bye." Because if a friendship isn't taking you closer to God's purpose, it's not for you. It's not true community and won't do your relationship any good either.

You might have giftings, callings, vision, but without godly community, you can't reach the purpose God has for you. You might have identified areas where you need healing and recovery, but without godly community, you might be struggling for a long time. The things we've been talking about in taking your relationship from good to great depend so often on what community can provide.

Maybe you feel like you're too busy to get in a community like a small group. I bet you *are* busy. But you may be busy with things that aren't pushing you toward your purpose or bringing healing and growth. Maybe it's time to break that cycle.

Maybe you say, "Well, I have a huge company." You still need community. A company is not a close faith group where you can be real about everything going on in your life.

"Well, I've been hurt in community before." God is a God of second chances.

"I just don't know if I'll be heard." If one group doesn't work, another one will.

Forget the excuses. You need fellowship like the early church did. And so does your loved one.

EVERY COUPLE NEEDS COMMUNITY. We quote Genesis that it's "not good for the man to be alone" (2:18). Well, let me tell you, it's not good for a couple to be alone either. You might be all in love and wrapped up in each other, but don't get so tight you forget your need for other people too. Every couple needs community.

DISCUSS

- Which friends and acquaintances do you need to divorce, and why?
- What would be the ideal type and level of involvement in Christian community for the two of you?

As a couple, commit to being part of a faith-based small group or other type of close community that meets regularly. If you're already in a community, discuss and write down how to maximize those relationships to build your couple relationship.

NOTES ON ISSUES WE DISCUSSED, PLANS WE MADE,
AND THINGS WE BELIEVE GOD IS SAYING TO US:

DAY 22 GET H.O.T.

Two people are better off than one, for they can
help each other succeed. If one person falls, the
other can reach out and help. But someone who
falls alone is in real trouble. Likewise, two people
lying close together can keep each other warm.
But how can one be warm alone? A person
standing alone can be attacked and defeated, but
two can stand back-to-back and conquer. Three
are even better, for a triple-braided cord is not
easily broken.

—ECCLESIASTES 4:9–12

One day I put together a new outfit to preach in. I asked my
wife, "How do I look?"

Natalie said, "Uh, the shirt's just a little tight around the
tum."

"Girl, please. This shirt ain't tight around my tum." But it
was. I'd put on a few pounds recently.

She said, "Come here. I'm going to cut a slit up the side so
that it doesn't pull."

That was a small thing. But see the power of this: I was
vulnerable enough to let her see things that I wouldn't show
others, and she saved me an hour of embarrassment.

My question for you is this: Are you open and vulnerable
with your closest loved ones and the godly community you've
got surrounding you?

You might say, "Oh, my bestie, she know everything." Or

"My brother and me, we're this close." But are you really telling the heaviest things that are weighing on you? Are you holding a piece back? Or worse, pretending things are better than they are? That ain't real. You can't have godly community with lies.

The Bible goes there. As we've already seen in some previous challenges, we're supposed to confess our sins to one another and pray for one another (James 5:16), and we're supposed to bear one another's burdens (Galatians 6:2). We can't do this unless we know what's going on in one another's lives. The good stuff. The hard stuff. The in-between stuff.

I'm not talking about spilling your guts about everything to everybody. That's what reality TV is for. I'm just saying that if you're in a romantic relationship, you need to be open and honest with your partner. And if you've got an inner circle, a godly community, they need to know things, too, if those things are important to you. At our church, we call it being H.O.T.—honest, open, and transparent.

H.O.T.— HONEST, OPEN, AND TRANSPARENT

Ecclesiastes 4:9 says, "Two people are better off than one, for they can help each other succeed." Your success is wrapped up with godly community. Yeah, maybe you're quiet, you're shy, you're reserved. Maybe you're embarrassed, worried about gossip, or don't think you're important enough for others to concern themselves about. Let me tell you something— you need other people.

You've probably heard the saying "There is no *I* in *team*." Where can you find an *I*? In *isolation*. And that's where the Enemy would like to keep us. Cut off, guarded, hurting in private.

Ecclesiastes continues, "If one person falls, the other can

reach out and help. But someone who falls alone is in real trouble" (verse 10). I've seen real trouble over and over again (including in my own life) when people live in isolation and don't find an appropriate place to share something that's going on.

RELATIONSHIPS FALL APART BECAUSE OTHERS DON'T SPEAK INTO THE SITUATION BEFORE IT GETS TOO BAD.

If people don't know what we're struggling with, they can't pray with us or direct us to Scripture or remind us we're not alone. If they don't know we're facing a big decision, they can't offer advice. Marriages and other romantic relationships fall apart because others don't speak into the situation before it gets too bad. Depression, lack of self-confidence, and other emotional afflictions flourish in isolation. Sin breeds under the cover of darkness.

But on the other hand, Ecclesiastes goes on to say, "A person standing alone can be attacked and defeated, but two can stand back-to-back and conquer" (verse 12). That's a picture of two soldiers defending against attacks coming from 360 degrees. It's the literal meaning of "I've got your back." You can't defend 360 degrees of territory on your own, and you shouldn't try. It takes two.

It's not about seeing eye to eye either. It's about standing back to back. The people we share our stuff with might not always see it the same way we do, but we can still fight together. This is the kind of unity the closest relationships need.

So, here is a call to reevaluate your openness in your relationship and in the godly community we started talking about yesterday. You're not a finished product. Don't pretend you've got it all together. Who gets to see you while you're still becoming who you're going to be?

DISCUSS

- Discuss what kinds of issues are appropriate to share with different people in your lives.
- Tell your relationship partner about an issue in your life that he or she doesn't know about.

Be prayer warriors for each other today, interceding with God for each other's needs. Go into it in faith, knowing Christ's side is the winning side and the Enemy is a loser.

NOTES ON ISSUES WE DISCUSSED, PLANS WE MADE,
AND THINGS WE BELIEVE GOD IS SAYING TO US:

DAY 23 GIVE IT UP

Submit to one another out of reverence for Christ.
For wives, this means submit to your husbands as to the Lord. . . .
For husbands, this means love your wives, just as Christ loved the church. He gave up his life for her to make her holy and clean, washed by the cleansing of God's word.

—EPHESIANS 5:21-22, 25-26

God is love, and love has an action that goes with it. We all know the scripture "For God so loved" that He did what? "He gave" (John 3:16, NIV). You will never see real love until there's real sacrifice of giving.

Most people these days want to take. They may not always say that out loud, but in their hearts they're wondering, *What can I get out of this relationship? What's in it for me?* You may have been hurt by this attitude in someone else, or you may have done the hurting.

In any case, that attitude should be something that a couple who care about each other should drop, especially if they have met at the altar to say, "I do."

The real mark of love is giving, and giving takes sacrifice. That's why Ephesians 5:25 says this for husbands: "Love your wives, just as Christ loved the church. He gave up his life for her." And wives are to submit to their husbands (verse 22). This is not aggressive, authoritarian dominance. This is having a mission and being "sub" to that mission. That's why I like to call this loving submission; it looks like what verse 21 says for both the husband and the wife—to "submit to one another."

> **THE REAL MARK OF LOVE IS GIVING, AND GIVING TAKES SACRIFICE.**

You want a real definition of marriage? It's a lot of dying to self. You wake up every morning and you die to yourself. What you want to do, your likes, your hopes for the day—you have to put some of them on hold for the sake of your spouse. But it's all for unity, and it's one of the most beautiful pictures because you become more like God and can give to somebody who doesn't want everything that you want.

If you're married or you're going to be married, God's purpose for the marriage is that you as a couple win in relationship. But it isn't a selfish-grab kind of thing. Love in marriage is sacrificial love. It's Christlike love. This is why I firmly believe that in the fullest sense, love doesn't really come until after marriage.

Jesus had some harsh things to say to people who made sure everybody saw it when they gave money to the poor, prayed, or fasted (Matthew 6). In the same way, you don't make sacrifices for your loved one to get noticed. You don't do it because you expect something in return. You do it because you love. It's often hidden. Or it's such a reflex that even *you* hardly notice it.

So, where do you make sacrifices in your relationship at times? In choosing what to eat? What to watch on television? Where to go on vacation? How to use your time? How to spend your money? Is it in cleaning up and doing chores? Putting up with annoying habits your spouse can't help? Postponing your own goals to make room for the other person to pursue his God-given purpose?

In one sense, these are little things. In another sense, they're huge!

I'd say sacrificing isn't just a relationship goal. It's a relationship necessity. A romantic relationship can never be what it's meant to be without sacrifice.

And yes, it can sometimes feel like we're sacrificing all the time, and we can get resentful. It's easy to slip into comparison (*Well, she hasn't been doing anything for me, so why should I do this for her?*). But stop right there! Don't grow weary in well doing (Galatians 6:9). Don't keep score (1 Corinthians 13:5). Remember Christ's example to you. Remember what it's all for. And pick up your cross again.

Meanwhile (hopefully), through your example and the Holy Spirit's leading, your partner will be sacrificial too. You'll benefit from her sacrifice, and you'll understand what it means because you're sacrificing too.

> MARRIAGE ISN'T A GIVE-AND-TAKE RELATIONSHIP. IT'S SOMETHING BETTER: IT'S A GIVE-AND-GIVE RELATIONSHIP.

Marriage isn't a give-and-take relationship. It's something better than that—it's a give-and-give relationship.

Look here, Christ's sacrifice won the prize of eternal life. Our sacrifice in marriage builds a unity that comes closer to re-presenting the bond between Christ and His people than any other human relationship ever could. Sacrifice is a key to winning in relationship *together*.

DISCUSS

- Ask whether there's something more your spouse or gf/bf needs from you.
- Express gratitude for the sacrificial things your loved one does for you.

Write down two things you can do that are valuable to your loved one and costly to you. Complete them today, and expect nothing in return.

NOTES ON ISSUES WE DISCUSSED, PLANS WE MADE, AND THINGS WE BELIEVE GOD IS SAYING TO US:

DAY 24   LOVE SPOKEN HERE

Most important of all, continue to show deep love for each other.

—1 PETER 4:8

More than seven thousand languages are spoken on the earth today. If you don't know the language spoken by someone you're trying to converse with, it doesn't matter how eloquent you are in your own language—the message won't get through.

> YOU MIGHT THINK YOU'RE COMMUNICATING YOUR LOVE TO YOUR PARTNER, BUT SHE MIGHT NOT SEE IT THAT WAY.

It can be the same way with love. You might think you're communicating your love to your partner, but she might not see it that way.

I often advise dating couples to read Gary Chapman's *The Five Love Languages*. Married couples should read it too. Chapman describes the love languages of physical touch, quality time, words of affirmation, acts of service, and gifts. He proposes that everyone has a primary way of giving and receiving love. If this interests you, you can take an online quiz to determine your love language.

But let me give you the headline: Chapman's right in his core idea. Many couples are speaking totally different love languages. They mean well; they just don't know any better.

Early on, Natalie and I didn't know any better. I thought that Natalie liked gifts, but actually her top two love languages are quality time and acts of service.

Before I knew this, I would buy Natalie a lot of gifts, like five pairs of shoes at one time. And she'd be like, "Oh, thank you."

I was like, "I just spent all this money, and all you can say is 'Oh, thank you'?"

She would much rather I spend time with her instead of spending the money at the store. Don't get me wrong—she likes gifts, just not as much as quality time.

Meanwhile, my top two love languages are physical touch and words of affirmation. On the quiz, you can score 1 through 12. Funny thing is, Natalie's highest score—quality time—is my lowest. She scored a 12 and I scored a 1. That doesn't mean that we aren't supposed to be together. That just means we have to work hard to communicate our love to each other in a way we both receive it.

For Natalie, words of affirmation didn't come naturally, so she had to come up with creative ways to speak that language. She actually checked on Pinterest to learn how to do this. As a result, she got Post-it notes and wrote words of affirmation on them, things like "You can champion your day" and "You are handsome." Then she put them on my mirror in the bathroom so, when I got ready for work, I could read those words that encouraged me, supported me, and affirmed me.

Getting in the habit of speaking each other's love language can stretch us and be downright hard, but the work is worth it. It can transform the satisfaction of your relationship by translating your love into a message that is received and understood.

You don't have to do Chapman's love languages assessment if you don't want to. But in that case I *do* strongly recommend you try to figure out on your own how to get the message of love through to your partner. Today's discussion and GO challenge will help.

DISCUSS

- As well as you know them, what are your love languages?
- What are some examples of ways you like your partner to speak those languages to you?

Before today is over, find at least one occasion to show love to your partner in a way that he or she most likes to receive it.

NOTES ON ISSUES WE DISCUSSED, PLANS WE MADE, AND THINGS WE BELIEVE GOD IS SAYING TO US:

DAY 25 FIGHTING FOR UNITY

Don't let the sun go down while you are still angry.

—EPHESIANS 4:26

If you're in a romantic relationship (especially marriage) with somebody, then you have some level of unity—yet at times you might *feel* disunited. You might *feel* misunderstood, angry, disrespected, overlooked, hurt. And if your feelings are out of sync with your oneness long enough, they can threaten to take away not only the joy of the relationship but even the relationship itself. You and I have both known too many marriages that started out full of smiles in front of a pastor and ended up full of anger and bitterness before a divorce judge.

That's why I think every couple should have a relationship goal of agreeing on what to do when they disagree so that their arguments don't leave lasting scars on their souls or create permanent cracks in their unity.

Let me see if I can fundamentally change how you think about fighting as a couple: What if you don't see it as fighting each other? What if you see it as fighting together against whatever disagreement or misunderstanding you have

> **AGREE ON WHAT TO DO WHEN YOU DISAGREE SO THAT ARGUMENTS DON'T LEAVE LASTING SCARS OR CREATE PERMANENT CRACKS IN YOUR UNITY.**

DON'T FIGHT EACH OTHER. FIGHT TOGETHER AGAINST WHATEVER DISAGREEMENT YOU HAVE UNTIL YOU RESTORE YOUR UNITY.

until you restore your unity? See the difference?

In Day 22, I described two soldiers fighting back to back (Ecclesiastes 4:12). That's a good picture for marital fighting. Sure, you need to look at each other face to face and work things out between you. But beneath that? You're fighting together against anything, coming from any direction, that would threaten your unity.

For this, you need to have a battle plan for fighting for unity. I'm talking about some rules. Some guidelines to which you both intend to stick.

In chapter 9 of *Relationship Goals,* Natalie and I get you started with two rules:

1. Cut out unspoken expectations.
2. Pay attention to your word choice and tone.

I tell the story of one day, early in our marriage, when Natalie and I stopped at a QuikTrip to get gas. I pumped the gas while Natalie went inside to get a snack. We'd been talking about how hot it was that day (the air-conditioning in our old van didn't work), so I'd assumed she would get a cold drink for me. I *assumed* that. I didn't say anything about it.

Natalie came out with one bottle of sweet tea (a drink I don't even like) and one doughnut. I lost it. I grabbed her doughnut and chucked it out the window, then put the van in gear and blew out of the parking lot.

It wasn't Natalie's fault. She didn't know I was expecting her to buy me a snack. That day we learned we needed to cut out unspoken expectations.

Also, the fact that I was so angry delayed our getting to the root of the problem. I don't remember my exact words in that van, but I said something like, "Nat, I can't believe you would just go in there and buy that one doughnut and that one bottle of sweet tea—which you know I don't even like—and not get anything for me! Is it too much to ask for you to think about me once in a while?"

It took us two days to resolve that conflict! If both of us had paid more attention to our word choice and tone, we could have gotten to the root of the problem sooner and worked it out. We could have moved on to understanding, forgiveness, reconciliation, and growth as a couple much faster.

Ephesians offers another guideline for dealing with anger: Don't put it off. Do it quickly. Get over your disagreement before bedtime so that if you're married, you can lie down in the marriage bed together with your love and unity restored. I wish Natalie and I had managed to get over our disagreement that quickly after the infamous QuikTrip incident.

Go online and google "fighting fair," and you'll come up with lots of blogs and such with suggested rules for arguing constructively instead of destructively. Or ask a mentor couple for their advice about fighting fair. What you find out might not necessarily all be wise or helpful to your relationship, but I bet you can find some insights you can use for today's challenge.

Most of all, though, remember the Third Member of your marriage triangle. Go to God in prayer every time your unity is threatened. He cemented your marriage covenant together in the first place. If you ask Him, He'll patch up the cracks as they appear along the way.

Fight well, and your unity could be stronger than ever.

DISCUSS

- What kinds of things tend to trigger your fights?
- What effect has your fighting had on your relationship?

With your loved one, agree on some of your rules as a couple for fighting for unity. Write them down.

NOTES ON ISSUES WE DISCUSSED, PLANS WE MADE, AND THINGS WE BELIEVE GOD IS SAYING TO US:

DAY 26 KINGDOM COWORKERS

Jesus came and told his disciples, "I have been given all authority in heaven and on earth. Therefore, go and make disciples of all the nations, baptizing them in the name of the Father and the Son and the Holy Spirit. Teach these new disciples to obey all the commands I have given you. And be sure of this: I am with you always, even to the end of the age."

—MATTHEW 28:18-20

When I talk about relationship goals, I like to emphasize that everybody has different purposes in life. It's true. I'm glad somebody's purpose is to teach kindergartners, somebody's purpose is to design computer code, and somebody's purpose is to build buildings, because we need all that—and those things definitely aren't in my makeup at all!

You and your relationship partner might have very different purposes from each other too. Maybe one of you was made for being an entrepreneur and the other for being a therapist.

But I've asked myself, *Is there anything that's a part of all our purposes?*

I think the answer is yes. In fact, Jesus gives us a clear picture of what He wants for you and me and all other believers, and it's found in today's scripture.

Now, let me give you some context.

Jesus died and was resurrected, and He had forty days on the earth to prepare His followers for life without Him after He ascended to heaven. What we see in these Matthew verses is the last conversation He had with His disciples.

What were His final instructions? He said to His disciples, "Go and make disciples." They were to *be* disciples, and they were to *make* disciples.

Okay, what is a disciple? I've heard it said that a disciple of Jesus is someone who learns from Him to live like Him.

This is not necessarily the same thing as being a Christian, at least not in the way we throw around the word *Christian* sometimes. Some people call themselves Christians because they go to church on Sunday, but they don't live as if Jesus matters to them from Monday through Saturday. Or they don't mind saying Jesus is a good spiritual example, like Buddha, Muhammad, and others, but they don't worship Jesus as Lord.

So the Great Commission is nothing like getting social media likes for Jesus. Y'all, Jesus was talking about making *disciples*—people who are prepared to follow Him with their whole lives. And die for His sake if it comes to that. This is serious.

> WHEN WE ARE DISCIPLES AND MAKE DISCIPLES, WE ARE A PART OF THE HISTORIC CHAIN OF FAITH REPRODUCTION INSIDE THE KINGDOM OF GOD.

When we are disciples and we make disciples, we are a part of the chain of faith reproduction that's been going on inside the kingdom of God throughout history. It's not some mere religious or feel-good experience.

Again, this is something we're all supposed to do. It's not just preachers like me. It's not just evangelists who speak to big crowds. Everybody who knows Jesus should be a part of this.

So, here's what I want to ask you today: Are you and your partner making disciples? And if your relationship has advanced far enough, are you doing it *together*?

Are you influencing people who are without faith to turn to Jesus?

Are you telling your own stories of transformation?

Are you passing on what you've learned about Jesus's teachings and His life?

In the Day 10 challenge I talked about how marriage represents the love of God for people. But at some point, we have to get more specific about pointing to Jesus. There are lots of ways to plant and water seeds of faith, but without all of us taking part, the harvest isn't going to be as abundant as it could be.

We make disciples because we want to obey Jesus's final commandment and because we love Him, but I'd like to point out a benefit in this that you might not have thought about. When two people are in a romantic relationship and they serve God together, this shared ministry brings them closer in a way nothing else can.

> **SERVING GOD TOGETHER IN SHARED MINISTRY BRINGS A COUPLE CLOSER IN A WAY NOTHING ELSE CAN.**

Natalie and I are copastors of our church. We've been side by side in ministry for years. Sometimes our church sees us up on stage together, but even when it's just me who's getting attention, you can be sure Natalie is involved 100 percent behind the scenes. I love it!

Out of our unity in the marriage covenant comes a super-

tight partnership in the gospel. And then our ministry together strengthens and blesses our marriage.

I'm not suggesting you need to be a pastor to have a ministry. Doing ministry is simply sharing the gospel everywhere
you go and in your sphere of influence. It's in the job description of every disciple of Christ.

Are you starting to get a sense of how you could have a
shared mission with your spouse or bf/gf that has eternal influence and earthly blessing?

DISCUSS

- How has God equipped the two of you to do ministry
  and service in Jesus's name?
- If you were to minister together as a couple, how do you
  think that would influence your relationship?

GO

Decide how the two of you will try to deliberately re-present
Christ to others today (or if not today, before the week is
out). Write down your intention.

NOTES ON ISSUES WE DISCUSSED, PLANS WE MADE,
AND THINGS WE BELIEVE GOD IS SAYING TO US:

DAY 27 INVESTMENT IN LOVE

Love is patient, love is kind. It does not envy, it does not boast, it is not proud. It does not dishonor others, it is not self-seeking, it is not easily angered, it keeps no record of wrongs. Love does not delight in evil but rejoices with the truth. It always protects, always trusts, always hopes, always perseveres.

Love never fails.

—1 CORINTHIANS 13:4–8, NIV

Today, my marriage with Natalie has more unity than I would ever have believed. I can clearly see the apostle Paul's description of love come true before my eyes.

But listen, y'all, it didn't just happen. It came from a lot of faithfulness, a lot of long conversations, a lot of fighting with tears in our eyes. But when we get to the tough spots, we both know we're not gonna quit. We're going to work this out.

A lot of people think, *Oh, you're going to lose so much when you get married.* But honestly, it's the investment you're making in that one relationship that causes you to gain so much.

I've found that, as I focus on Natalie daily, as I focus on my relationship with God daily, as I focus on what I need to grow in and who I am daily, I'm inching my way to this version of myself that I didn't even know was there. Years ago, I was a liar, addicted to pornography, a manipulator. I cheated on Natalie before we got married. Today, I'm faithful, romantic, and thoughtful. That's not a boast, because it's not like one day I woke up and I was like, *Oh, now I'm all these things I wished.* It was slow progress under the mercy of God.

> IT'S THE INVESTMENT YOU'RE MAKING IN THAT ONE RELATIONSHIP THAT CAUSES YOU TO GAIN SO MUCH.

I think too many people give up on love and unity too quickly. Like I've heard it said, they overestimate what they can do in one year and they underestimate what they can do in ten. If people would stay in a relationship instead of giving up and throwing in the towel, they would be so surprised what they could do in a decade.

From our ministry, to our children, to our love, to our finances, to our friendships—everything ten years ago was nothing like it is today. But it all *was* there in seed form. And that's why I tell everybody, "You can never compare your planted seed to somebody's tree. It will only make you feel discouraged. But if you keep watering that seed and you keep rejoicing and celebrating every time you see just the little progression, then one day it will be a tree covered with fruit."

Natalie and I got married in 2010. Recently, to celebrate our tenth anniversary, we had a vow renewal ceremony. (If you're married and that sounds like a fun thing to do, I'm going to give you a hint right now: you might want to flip to the back of this book and look at Day 31.) I would like to quote here what I said to Natalie on that occasion:

In 2010, I got life. It was when I made the decision to marry you. And as I stood there ten years ago saying all these vows that I hoped would be true—for richer and poorer, in sickness and in health, till death do us part— back then it was a hope. Ten years later, this is a guarantee from me: I'm going to be with you until there's no more sun. I'm going to be with you until I see Jesus. I'm going to be with you if we have everything or if we have nothing.

As I think about our three beautiful children getting to see this relationship goal that we have, this has not been about perfection at all. It's been about progression. And I would not be the man I am today without you. Every success I have ever had was built on the foundation of our love. Every blessing that I've ever received has been because God somehow favored me when He gave me you.

Today, ten years later, I want to let you know, I still do. And I will always. I can see my future in your eyes. You really are my future forever.

I pray every night and I thank God every morning for the day that you came into my life. And as I think about you being cut open three times for us to have children and the sacrifice that you make continually for us to touch the world, there is not one person in this world that I would rather give my all to than you. I choose you. I chose you and I'll always choose you.

I love you forever. For another hundred years, I'm going to be your man.

Make the sacrifice for love and unity. In the long run, it's worth it!

DISCUSS

- How are you investing in your romantic relationship?
- If you look at the seeds of your relationship right now, what do you hope they might one day grow to be?

Talk with your loved one about what is the highest-impact investment you could make in the long-term growth and strength of your relationship. Start pouring your energy and devotion into that.

NOTES ON ISSUES WE DISCUSSED, PLANS WE MADE,
AND THINGS WE BELIEVE GOD IS SAYING TO US:

DAY 28 COMMITTED TO THE RIDE

Wherever you go, I will go; wherever you live, I
will live. Your people will be my people, and your
God will be my God. Wherever you die, I will die,
and there I will be buried.

—RUTH 1:16–17

Let me start out today with a roller-coaster analogy. (Why
not?) What do you see at the head of a line of people waiting
to get on a big, scary roller coaster? Some people are excited
and can't wait for the ride. But others are saying, "No way!
I'm not going to do it. Get me out of here!" Maybe they cut
out of the line or maybe they don't. One way or another,
when it's their turn, they've got to either commit to the ride or
not.

I hope you'll forgive me for comparing a romantic relationship, in particular marriage, to a big, scary roller-coaster
ride—but you've got to admit, there are some similarities.
When you're looking ahead to marriage, you don't know exactly what it's going to be like. You expect it to be fun, but
you know it's going to have dips and turns coming out of
nowhere. You can hear people ahead of you on the ride, and
they're screaming their heads off. Do you really want to go on
a ride that makes people shout in terror?

Well, if you said "I do," then you are already committed to
the ride of marriage. If you're engaged, you could still back
out, but even in that case you've already made a public prom-

ise. You're almost to the point of strapping into the seat on the Covenant of Marriage Ride of Your Life.

But think about this. Actually, *all* important relationships require a commitment of some kind.

What about Ruth when she committed to the ride of going back to Israel with her mother-in-law? Naomi said, "You don't have to do this. Think twice, girl."

But Ruth was ready. And people are still quoting her commitment: "Wherever you go, I will go; wherever you live, I will live. Your people will be my people, and your God will be my God. Wherever you die, I will die, and there I will be buried."

When Elijah called Elisha to become a prophet, Elisha used his wooden plow as firewood to cook the oxen he'd been plowing with. This feast showed that his days as a farmer were over and done with (1 Kings 19:21).

Or what about the apostles when Jesus called them to follow? We know they were committed because "they left their nets at once and followed him" (Matthew 4:20). Their nets were the symbol of their old livelihood. Now they were embarking with Jesus on a new career as fishers of men and women.

When it comes to marriage, Jesus said, "Let no one split apart what God has joined together" (Matthew 19:6). It's a lifelong deal. As much as people are making fake marriages by living together without covenant, and as much as they are taking advantage of easy divorce laws to marry again and again, the plan from the start was that a man and a woman would commit to marriage once and for all.

The thing is, when you're in marriage, there can come times during the dips and turns of the ride that you wonder whether the other person is really still committed. Is he secretly thinking about bailing from the relationship? Is he just gutting it out but doesn't really want to be there anymore?

FROM TIME TO TIME, WE NEED TO HEAR THAT THE OTHER PERSON STILL LOVES US AND WANTS TO BE IN RELATIONSHIP WITH US.

From time to time, we need to hear that the other person still loves us and wants to be in relationship with us, despite the barrel roll of bankruptcy, the corkscrew of parenting, the dark tunnel of illness, the free fall of sin, or whatever other thrills and chills the ride throws at us. We're strapped in, and we're staying put till the end.

And do you want to know something else? The Third Member of the marriage—God—is totally and unchangeably committed to both of you.

DISCUSS

- What parts of marriage do you think make it seem most risky?
- How important is it to you for your partner to assure you of his or her commitment? Why?

GO

If you are in a committed romantic relationship, write out a statement assuring your partner of your continued faithfulness and commitment. Read your statements to each other.

NOTES ON ISSUES WE DISCUSSED, PLANS WE MADE,
AND THINGS WE BELIEVE GOD IS SAYING TO US:

DAY 29   NEVER PAUSE ON PURSUIT

"At last!" the man exclaimed.

"This one is bone from my bone,
   and flesh from my flesh!
She will be called 'woman,'
   because she was taken from 'man.'"

This explains why a man leaves his father and
mother and is joined to his wife, and the two are
united into one.

—GENESIS 2:23–24

It's hard to beat the King James Version of verse 24: "Therefore shall a man leave his father and his mother, and shall cleave unto his wife: and they shall be one flesh." There's the *leaving* and the *cleaving*. A man and a woman *separate* from their families of origin and then *unite* to form a new family. Having a relationship goal means going through transformation, and this is the number one transformation most single people are looking for.

But if you go to a Hebrew dictionary and look up the word translated as "cleave" (old-timey Bible) or "is joined to" (modern Bible), you'll find something interesting. A part of its meaning is "to pursue closely." Marriage and commitment are not just about oneness. They are also about pursuit.

Some couples seem to have lost that idea. They sort of sit on the couch and say, "We together now. Here we are. I got him. I got her. We all booed up, so what more is there?"

If that's your attitude, you'll stop pursuing your significant other. And the love and the fun and the forward motion as a couple are going to vanish real soon. This is particularly an issue for married couples.

Let me tell you something—"I do" is *not* the destination of a marriage.

What is the destination? It's "death do us part." It's the whole marriage, for as long as you both shall live.

Think of the wedding as the starting line, not the finish line. The wedding is just the beginning of cultivating the relationship, helping each other develop into who you are meant to be,

> **THINK OF THE WEDDING AS THE STARTING LINE, NOT THE FINISH LINE.**

showing support and love, meeting each other's needs, and focusing on God together. These are things you can keep working on and getting better at through all the seasons of life you've got left.

So never pause on pursuing your loved one. If you're not married yet but you're in a relationship, establish that habit of pursuit now. If you're married, keep on pursuing. Men might usually take the lead here, but women, too, can find ways of showing they still care.

I told you back in the introduction that I wouldn't be giving you a lot of cheesy relationship hacks, but hey, there come times for things like this:

- Spontaneously hug or say, "I love you."
- Give a thoughtful gift.
- Tell your loved one how you feel about her.
- Text to let your loved one know you're thinking about him.

- Write a love note.
- Ask about her day.
- Do a chore with your partner.

I love Natalie more today than I ever have because she has continued to change and I've continued to pursue her through all the changes. I give her the signs she's looking for that she's in my heart for good.

Everyone wants to feel loved and wanted. Continuing the pursuit is one of the best things you and your partner can do for each other. (More on this in the next, and final, challenge.)

DISCUSS

- Tell your partner about one or more ways he or she has pursued you in the past that you really appreciate.
- If you were to re-create one of your favorite dates of the past, what would it be?

Before the day is out, give your loved one a tangible sign of affection to show that you still love, like, and are interested in him or her.

NOTES ON ISSUES WE DISCUSSED, PLANS WE MADE,
AND THINGS WE BELIEVE GOD IS SAYING TO US:

DAY 30 YOU'RE SO FRESH!

Place me like a seal over your heart,
   like a seal on your arm.
For love is as strong as death,
   its jealousy as enduring as the grave.
Love flashes like fire,
   the brightest kind of flame.
Many waters cannot quench love,
   nor can rivers drown it.

—SONG OF SOLOMON 8:6-7

With three kids and a ministry that God keeps blessing like crazy, we are busy. Many times in recent years, Natalie and I have had to revisit our priorities and make changes to our calendars. Frankly, some things that were good but not crucial have just had to go.

But one thing Natalie and I are holding on to is our regular dates. It would be so easy to get careless about that. But nope, we won't do it.

Every week we have a date night. We swap who plans the date each week. Sometimes it's an extravagant date experience; other times it's just watching TV on the couch. But whatever it is, we don't miss it.

I tell single people to do intentional dating, not recreational dating. Their goals should be to get to know the other person and find out if the two of them are meant for each other. (See chapter 4 of *Relationship Goals*.)

Well, even if you've already got a partner, you should still do intentional dating. But here the goal is *reconnecting*. Going out on dates keeps the relationship fresh. You're reminded of why you got married in the first place. You're reminded of the fact that there's actu-

> GOING OUT ON DATES KEEPS THE RELATION-SHIP FRESH.

ally life apart from kids, work, bills, social media, and piles of laundry. Dating keeps life fun. It keeps the relationship vibrant and the romance going.

I'm not trying to tell you that continuing to date when you've been together awhile is going to be a solution to all your problems or make you as giddy as newlyweds. But I will say this: if you *don't* work to keep connected by spending special time together, it's guaranteed your relationship is headed for trouble.

So, get ready—*I'm coming to your house.*

When was the last time you took your partner out on a date? Don't just be with your mate, chillin', watching movies. What happened to the pursuit? What happened to showing interest? Finding out more about each other? Like I said— reconnecting?

Recommit to dating. It's okay to do your favorite thing over and over, like dinner and a movie, if that's what you want. But since we're talking about keeping your relationship fresh, why not keep your dating practices fresh as well? Do any of these sound good?

- Try a new restaurant in town or one that offers a type of cuisine you've never tasted before.
- Go horseback riding.

- If you usually go to one type of music concerts (like pop or hip-hop), try a different kind (like jazz or classical).
- Take dance classes together.
- Take a walk at a botanical garden.
- Sculpt or paint together. (The result doesn't have to be gallery worthy.)
- Go see the new exhibit at the museum.
- Visit a comedy club.
- Work out together, like taking a long bike ride.
- Do something that will get the adrenaline flowing, like bungee jumping or rock climbing.
- Go to an arcade or amusement park.
- Have a picnic outdoors.
- Go ice skating or roller skating.

You'll keep changing as you grow older. So will your partner. You'll have new dreams and goals. So will your partner. You chose this person because you believed he would be a godly support, and if you're married, both of you need a marriage that continues to be mutually supportive, with or without kids in the house. So keep it fresh and go on regular dates. Renew the relationship so that it remains close and rewarding.

DISCUSS

- How can the two of you make regular dating work in your schedules?
- What are some new things you'd like to try on a date? Go!

To reconnect—and celebrate completing the thirty-day challenge!—go out on a special date with your sweetheart. Talk. Laugh. Hold hands. Look into each other's eyes.

TIP: Hold on to this book and revisit the notes you've written.

NOTES ON ISSUES WE DISCUSSED, PLANS WE MADE,
AND THINGS WE BELIEVE GOD IS SAYING TO US:

GO LIST

DAY 1. Spend time in prayer together with your significant other, inviting God to take control of your relationship and to guide and bless you in it.

DAY 2. Make plans for (or reevaluate) devotional practices that you have with your loved one.

DAY 3. With love, and in godly confidence, affirm the identity that God has given your loved one.

DAY 4. Make a plan to change what you need to change in your lives and relationship if you are going to go all out in pursuing God's calling.

DAY 5. Encourage your partner to say yes to whatever God is calling him or her to do right now. Also, keep your partner accountable for follow-through.

DAY 6. Together with your partner, decide the people you will go to when you need godly advice that affects how you live out your purpose.

DAY 7. Tell your loved one who you believe he or she can become through Christ. Make this a habit from now on.

DAY 8. Dream about ways you can develop the gifts and interests God has placed in you. Share these dreams with your partner. Ask for your partner's support in your plans for personal growth.

DAY 9. Pray with your loved one, asking for God's guidance in one or more decisions you've got to make.

DAY 10. Talk with your spouse about how your relationship can be a better witness to others of Christ's love.

DAY 11. Identify ways that God is calling you and your partner to trust in Him in the midst of your struggles.

DAY 12. Give your loved one realistic yet faithful encouragement in an area that you know is hard for him or her now.

DAY 13. If your partner is struggling with doubt, give support and encouragement to turn to God.

DAY 14. If you and your loved one can agree on what God is calling you to do to prepare for a miracle in your relationship, make a plan for being faithful to do it.

DAY 15. If you've been letting an emotional wound fester, identify something you can do to begin or speed up the healing process. It will help you and your relationship!

DAY 16. If you've been expecting your loved one to do something for you that only God can do, apologize to your partner. And commit to seeking God for healing instead.

DAY 17. Pray as a couple, asking God to build up the faith He's already given you. Thank Him for the joy that comes from being in Jesus.

DAY 18. Say nothing critical to your partner all day. Use edifying speech only. And let this day be a model for the future.

DAY 19. Make a secret plan for surprising your loved one with a better outcome in an area where you've been falling short. Shh, don't tell! But *do* follow through!

DAY 20. If you can do it sincerely, say the words "I forgive you." And let it go.

DAY 21. As a couple, commit to being part of a faith-based small group or other type of close community that meets regularly. If you're already in a community, discuss how to maximize those relationships to build your couple relationship.

DAY 22. Be prayer warriors for each other today, interceding with God for each other's needs. Go into it in faith, knowing Christ's side is the winning side and the Enemy is a loser.

DAY 23. Write down two things you can do that are valuable to your loved one and costly to you. Complete them today, and expect nothing in return.

DAY 24. Before today is over, find at least one occasion to show love to your partner in a way that he or she most likes to receive it.

DAY 25. With your loved one, agree on some of your rules as a couple for fighting for unity.

DAY 26. Decide how the two of you will try to deliberately re-present Christ to others today (or if not today, before the week is out).

DAY 27. Talk with your loved one about what is the highest-impact investment you could make in the long-term growth and strength of your relationship. Start pouring your energy and devotion into that.

DAY 28. If you are in a committed romantic relationship, write out a statement assuring your partner of your continued faithfulness and commitment. Read your statements to each other.

DAY 29. Before the day is out, give your loved one a tangible sign of affection to show that you still love, like, and are interested in him or her.

DAY 30. To reconnect—and celebrate completing the thirty-day challenge!—go out on a special date with your sweetheart. Talk. Laugh. Hold hands. Look into each other's eyes.

TIP: Hold on to this book and revisit the notes you've written.

DAY 31 BONUS CHALLENGE

In June 2020, Natalie and I celebrated our tenth wedding anniversary by renewing our wedding vows. (To see it for yourself, go to the Represent TV channel on YouTube and search for "10 Year Vow Renewal.") I think I might have had more fun with it than our original wedding—definitely I was less nervous!

If you're married, I've got a bonus challenge for you. Number 31 is to hold a wedding vow renewal ceremony of your own. Not just any wedding vow renewal ceremony but one that reaffirms the marriage triangle and puts your relationship goals firmly in the hands of God.

From what we learned by our experience, let me suggest these tips:

- Keep it simple, personal, and meaningful. Obviously, it will take some work, but don't turn it into such a big production that it's a burden to you.
- Pick a date and a place.
- Ask someone to preside. This isn't a legal event, so you can choose anyone you want to officiate.
- Plan the guest list and send out invitations. Include family

members, close friends, and the small group or godly community that supports your spiritual lives.

- Pick your clothes. You can do a tux-and-long-dress thing if you want, or it can be more casual.
- Choose the decorations and flowers. (Simple and inexpensive is fine.)
- Plan the ceremony itself. Your officiant may be able to help with this, or you can find plenty of wedding vow renewal scripts online. Choose music that honors God. Include prayer and Scripture reading.
- Write your own vows, reflecting in a positive way your experience in marriage and your recommitment to each other.
- Include with your vows a recommitment from you both to putting the Third Member of your marriage at the center of the relationship.
- You don't need new wedding rings, but you might ask your officiant to bless the rings.
- Decide whether you want a reception afterward. Casual and fun is the way to go.
- Make it a no-gift event.
- Record the ceremony and post the video on social media as a way of re-presenting Christ's love to others. You might include a direct challenge to those watching the video to learn to craft their own relationship goals around God's plan.
- Don't look at this as just a party. Consider it a fresh beginning in your ongoing pursuit of each other and of God.
- Go on a second honeymoon afterward. I mean, why not?

ABOUT THE AUTHORS

MICHAEL TODD is the lead pastor of Transformation Church in Tulsa, Oklahoma, and the *New York Times* bestselling author of *Relationship Goals*. His driving passion is re-presenting God to the lost and found for transformation in Christ. Michael speaks at a variety of influential churches, events, and conferences each year, including Elevation Church, C3 Conference, Lakewood Church, VOUS Conference, Relentless Church, XO Conference, and many others. Michael and his wife, Natalie, have been married since 2010 and live in Tulsa with their three children.

ERIC STANFORD is a writer and editor living in Monument, Colorado. He and his wife, Elisa, have two daughters.

Win in Relationships!

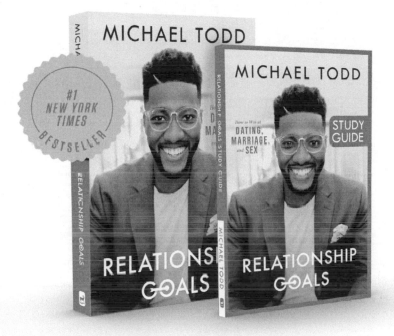

**Read it together and go deeper
in your relationships together!
Perfect for couples and small groups!**

RELATIONSHIP GOALS

#RelationshipGoals

WATERBROOK | IAmMikeTodd.com